Cryptocurrency Investor
Step by Step Guide to Making Money Trading Bitcoin and Altcoin

Table of Contents

INTRODUCTION TO CRYPTO INVESTING

Trust and the financial system

THE BASICS: WHAT IS CRYPTOCURRENCY

Understanding Cryptocurrency
Cryptocurrency vs stocks
Why Do I Need Crypto?
Opportunities in Cryptocurrency
A Short History of Cryptocurrency
Bitcoin and the Modern Cryptocurrency Boom
Blockchain & DeFi Explained
How Does the Blockchain Work?
Crypto Mining & Cloud Mining
ICO (Initial Coin Offering)

DIFFERENT TYPES OF CRYPTOCURRENCIES

Coins
Tokens
Stablecoins
Altcoins

POPULAR CRYPTOCURRENCIES

Bitcoin
Ethereum
Cardano
Ripple XRP
Solana
Dogecoin
Litecoin
Polygon / Matic
Binance Coin
Shiba Inu coin
Tether
Monero
Polkadot
USD Coin

Terra (Luna)
Avalanche
Chainlink
Other Altcoins

STORE CRYPTO IN WALLETS

Hot Storage Wallet
Cold Storage Wallet
Private/ Public Keys
Keep Crypto safe

HANDLE CRYPTO

How to buy
How to sell
How to send and receive crypto

CRYPTO INVESTING AND TRADING

How to invest in cryptocurrency
Cryptocurrency investment strategy
How to trade cryptocurrency
Cryptocurrency trading strategy
How to profit from crypto
What to avoid

CRYPTO STRATEGIES

Pick the right coin for you
Grow your profits and cut your losses
Follow the trend
Do not follow the crowd blindly
Know the basics for trading
Build a diversified crypto portfolio
When to sell
Do not fight the whales
What does HODL mean? Long term investment
Coin Staking
Crypto day trading
Special Deals

BASICS OF CRYPTO ANALYSIS

Why learn to read charts
Technical analysis for beginners
Trend lines
Supports and resistances
Moving Averages
Fundamentals
Things to look out for: Value, Market cap & dilution
Market cycles

CRYPTO AND THE REST OF THE WORLD

Taxes on Crypto
Applicability in Society
Popular Trading Apps & Platforms
Safety: Avoid Crypto Scams & Tips on Security

NFT

What is it (NFT vs. Crypto)?
How to create
How to buy & sell
Biggest marketplaces

WORLDWIDE DEVELOPMENTS

OUTLOOK AND CONCLUSION

Introduction to Crypto Investing

Welcome to the world of cryptocurrency!

Cryptocurrency is still an emerging topic, and there is a lot of misinformation out there. This book will set you on your way to become a confident investor in cryptocurrencies. This book is dedicated to long-term investment and realistic trading goals. If you're looking to get rich quick by promoting an obscure altcoin on social media, this might be the wrong book for you. The next step for you will be to decide what kind of investor you want to be.

What is cryptocurrency? Why should you buy it?! Which coin should you invest in? What about mining!? All of these questions and more will be answered in this book. The goal is to become an informed investor (or trader).

Note: Cryptocurrencies are here to stay, which means blockchain technology is as well! Blockchain technology will change the world as we know it. It can be difficult to keep up with what you need to know about cryptocurrency, Bitcoin, Ethereum and altcoins because of all the noise out there. The goal of this book is to cut the noise and lift the veil of mystery surrounding this new asset class. We will provide you with information that is not readily available on your own if you don't know where to look for it, or worse yet, incorrect information.

Before we start, a few words on the author. My name is Dillon Samuel and I am a cryptocurrency investor, enthusiast and writer. I started writing this book because of my passion for the topic. In fact, I have been investing in cryptocurrency for a few years now and have had a lot of success with my investments. However, in my opinion it is important to keep it cool and level-headed. I have invested in many different coins; some were successful and some were not. By blindly jumping on the hype train, you might as well be burning your money!

What I want to do is help new investors make informed decisions and therefore avoid pitfalls. It's a wild world out there, but one with a lot of opportunity. Just remember, it goes both ways – don't buy meme coins at all-time highs and do your own research before investing in anything.

The cryptocurrency market is still very active and developing and it is operational around the clock, seven days a week. This means that you will face rapid developments in this market and you will face different obstacles to overcome. You need to evolve together with the market in order to keep up with these advancements. It is vital that you stay abreast of the news and follow the market closely, as well as follow the upcoming trends in this market. You will need to be alert because developments can happen overnight.

As a new investor starting out with cryptocurrency investment, I remember how confused I was when I first started out. I felt like a fish out of water, trying to swim upstream in the river only to be swept away by strong currents and rapids. There were countless questions running through my mind. There was a lot of information on the internet, but it seemed fragmented and incomplete for me. I had no idea how to make sense of all this information as well as connect all the pieces together. All this time, I kept on asking myself: "How can I make some real money from investing in cryptocurrencies?". I felt like a beggar trying to get out of poverty and into wealth. I went from one website to another, from one book on cryptocurrency investment to another, from one seminar on how to make money with cryptocurrencies to another in hopes of finding the answer. But still no luck...

It was after this fruitless attempt that I realized I had to first put a solid foundation on what I was going to build upon. I had to build a strong base before going further and this is where the journey began. I discovered that the best place to start is at the very beginning. I had to learn what exactly cryptocurrencies were, how it worked, what its purpose was and why people invested in them. It has been an exhilarating experience for me - one filled with both excitement and pain; but most of all, it helped me discover my passion for this new industry. I am now here to share my expertise and experience with you so that you too can learn the basics of this industry and benefit from it, just as I did.

So, let's get to it!

Trust and the financial system

The world is changing at a rapid pace and we can hardly keep up with all the technological advancements. You can't expect to keep up with the times if you don't learn anything new. If you're not open-minded and continue to learn, you'll deteriorate as the world advances. This is true in many aspects of our life, and it is especially true in our personal financial situations. For starters, paper money is no longer widely used. Cash is inconvenient. When you think about it, using cash to pay for expenses and comforts is far more difficult than using a credit or debit card. You'll almost certainly agree that paying with the plastic card provided by your bank to pay for our items and pleasures is more convenient than paying in cash. Furthermore, this cashless transfer is also safer and more secure.

Humanity has just discovered a brand-new kind of money - digital money, sometimes known as cryptocurrency - that is still in its infancy. Cryptocurrency is created by the application of encryption software, and cryptocurrency units are generated and maintained using algorithmic encryption. This book will explain how crypto can be used to solve certain problems and how it works. However, for the moment, I'd want you to consider a concept known as trust. It's a major problem that cryptocurrencies like bitcoin aim to address.

Allow me to illustrate with an example from my own experience. When I was in school, I made the decision that I wanted to start a business and earn some money. Well, a business in a small scale, three of my classmates and I started to sell candy at our school. Our sales were recorded in a used vocabulary book, which we then passed on to each other. One day this vocabulary book was in my bag, and I was in desperate need of something sweet. I pondered whether or not I could change the recorded figures for my own benefit. However, I scolded myself and asked aloud what would happen if my pals did the same thing. As a result, even among the closest of friends, suspicion may develop. Because cryptocurrencies do not allow us to add or modify anything after it has been entered into the system, this problem is completely avoided. It is impossible to change the amount of money that was transferred between two parties after it has been completed.

Of course, this system also works in other situations, like when you're trying to transfer cash between two people who are strangers or don't trust each other. You can go ahead and pay your bills online without worrying about identity theft because your personal information will be protected. It is important to remember that this system has been in existence for a very long time, and the value of digital currencies like bitcoin has finally begun to gain mainstream acceptance.

Just like paper money, you can save your coins offline on what is called hardware wallets or paper wallets. This will prevent it from getting lost or stolen, and you won't need to worry about anyone hacking into your account online when buying or selling cryptocurrencies.

It's easy to start, but it can also be difficult because cryptocurrencies are not just another fad that will pass. Instead, they are the future of money. If you want to get in early before everyone starts jumping on the bandwagon, this is the book for you. Cryptocurrencies are growing in value by the day, and if you don't learn about them now, it may be too late when you finally realize what's going on.

The Basics: What is Cryptocurrency

While reading this book, your first question is undoubtedly, "What the heck is a cryptocurrency, exactly?" Simply stated, a cryptocurrency is a new form of digital money that has recently emerged. You may send regular, non-cryptocurrency money like the Dollar or Euro online, but this isn't the same as how cryptocurrencies operate. You'll be able to use them to pay for things and services exactly the same as you would with conventional money after cryptocurrencies become more widely accepted. The key difference is the technology that cryptocurrencies are based on. "What difference does it make what technology supports my money? My one and only worry is how much money I have in my pocket right now!" might be your next thought. The problem is that the world's current monetary systems are rife with problems.

Cryptocurrencies are designed to address at least some of these issues, if not all of them. The principles of cryptography are covered in this chapter. You're probably aware of how your regular, government-issued money is kept in a bank account. You should also be aware that in order to access your funds, you'll need an ATM or a banking portal. With cryptocurrency, you may be able to completely eliminate the need for banks and other centralized intermediaries in your transactions. This is due to the fact that cryptocurrencies are based on a technology known as blockchain, which is decentralized (meaning no single entity is in charge of it). The transactions are instead confirmed by each and every machine connected to the network.

When you sold your chicken for a pair of shoes in ancient times, the values of the things you were exchanging were inherent in their nature. However, when coins, cash, and credit cards entered the picture, the concept of money, and, more crucially, the trust model of money, were transformed. Another significant development in money has been the ease with which it may be transferred. One of the primary motivations for the invention of currency was the difficulty of transporting a metric ton of gold bars from one nation to another. Then, as individuals became even more sluggish, the invention of credit cards was made possible. Credit cards, on the other hand, contain money that is under the jurisdiction of your government.

Bitcoin and other cryptocurrencies may prove to be a viable alternative to traditional currencies as the globe grows more linked and people become more worried about authorities who may or may not have their best interests at heart. In the digital or virtual money world, a cryptocurrency is a digital or virtual currency that is protected by encryption, making it almost difficult to counterfeit or double spend. Many cryptocurrencies are decentralized networks based on blockchain technology—a distributed ledger maintained by a distant network of computers—which is used by a large number of cryptocurrencies to operate. Because cryptocurrencies are not issued by any central authority, they are theoretically resistant to meddling or manipulation by governments. This is one of the most distinguishing characteristics of cryptocurrency.

Bitcoin and other cryptocurrencies may prove to be a viable alternative to traditional currencies as the globe grows more linked and people become more worried about authorities who may or may not have their best interests at heart. In the digital or virtual money world, a cryptocurrency is a digital or virtual currency that is protected by encryption, making it almost difficult to counterfeit or double spend. Many cryptocurrencies are decentralized networks based on blockchain technology—a distributed ledger maintained by a distant network of computers—which is used by a large number of cryptocurrencies to operate. Because cryptocurrencies are not issued by any central authority, they are theoretically resistant to meddling or manipulation by governments. This is one of the most distinguishing characteristics of cryptocurrency.

In the digital asset world, a cryptocurrency is a digital asset that is created by a network of computers that is dispersed among a large number of nodes. As a result of their decentralized nature, they are able to exist independently of governments and other central authority. The term "cryptocurrency" is derived from the encryption methods that are used to protect the network from unauthorized access and usage. Blockchains, which are organizational systems for preserving the integrity of transactional data, are a critical component of many cryptocurrencies, and they are used to secure the transactions itself. Many experts predict that blockchain and associated technologies will have a significant impact on a wide range of businesses, including financial and legal services. Cryptocurrencies have come under fire for a variety of reasons, including their usage in unlawful activities, the volatility of their exchange rates, and the weaknesses of the infrastructure that underpins them. However, its mobility, divisibility, inflation resistance, and transparency have all been lauded as positive characteristics.

Understanding Cryptocurrency

Digital currencies, often known as cryptocurrency, are online payment systems that are priced in terms of virtual "tokens," which are represented by ledger entries stored inside the system's internal ledger. Crypto refers to the numerous encryption methods and cryptographic approaches that protect these entries, such as elliptical curve encryption, public-private key pairs, and hashing functions, all of which are defined as follows: It is time to redirect our focus away from fiat currencies, which are not genuine money when compared to gold, and towards cryptocurrencies, which are far more similar to gold than money as we know it now, and which would function better than fiat currencies if they were to be used instead.

The transfer of cryptocurrencies between accounts is easier than the transfer of fiat money and may be accomplished via the use of internet devices such as computers, tablets, and smartphones. When dealing with fiat money, you'll have to do it in person or via the same bank. Furthermore, since they are kept on the Internet, you will not be required to physically transport them with you. Consequently, you may go anywhere with a reliable Internet connection and carry your cryptocurrencies with you, regardless of their value. An asset may only be considered excellent value storage if it has the ability to maintain basically constant levels of usefulness or pleasure over a long period of time.

One of the explanations - although a superficial one - is the hue of cryptocurrency tokens in comparison to traditional money. Bitcoins are represented aesthetically as the color gold, while Litecoins are represented visually as the color silver. However, there are more than just visual indications to support the idea in cryptocurrencies' potential to hold value in the same way as the two most valuable metals on the planet do. Both asset classes are based on behavioral economics, which should not be dismissed as such. When more and more individuals begin to believe that cryptocurrencies such as Bitcoin, Ether, or Litecoin are capable of storing value in the same way that precious metals such as gold and silver are, the values of these cryptocurrencies may begin to rise.

The likelihood that they will be able to retain or increase their values over time is quite high when their prices do rise over time over an extended period. A highly powerful aspect that might impact the viewpoint of general markets on Bitcoin's and altcoin's ability to hold or store value over time is comparisons to precious metals, such as gold. For example, Bitcoins are often compared to gold. And this has the potential to have a significant influence on the amount of investors who consider cryptocurrencies in general to be excellent investment vehicles in the future. Cryptocurrencies are similar to gold in that they are, by their very nature, decentralized and self-sufficient.

This implies that, similar to gold, government actions or policy changes have little or no direct influence on their long-term values, if any at all, on their prices. One of the most heated debate topics among cryptocurrency users and investors is the degree of decentralization and autonomy desired. Some prefer complete autonomy, while others prefer some form of compromise, such as hybrid combinations of some form of governance (other than that provided by the government) and decentralization, which is acceptable to both parties involved. As a general rule, cryptocurrency governance models may be quite diverse, with some selecting a balanced power structure among its users when it comes to important decision-making on the one hand, and others opting for the benign dictatorship model on the other. In between the two extremes, there exist a variety of additional combination or hybrid versions. Although cryptocurrencies with more decentralized systems may be a better risk in terms of hedging against the possibility of their values being affected or tampered with by authorities, this is not always the case.

Cryptocurrency vs stocks

While it's true that some cryptocurrencies behave like stocks, you have to remember that they are very different. Cryptocurrencies tend to move more independently from the stock market and there is a clear distinction between cryptocurrencies and stocks.

The best way to think about cryptocurrencies is as a completely new asset class. Investing in cryptocurrency requires a lot of research because most cryptocurrencies behave like start-ups, since most are very early-stage projects. While some are clearly scams, the majority are legitimate projects that will affect our daily lives in a meaningful way.

Why Do I Need Crypto?

When you suggested the phrase "cryptocurrency" to someone a few years ago, many people immediately thought of some kind of currency involving an underground banking system, with hooded traders sitting behind shady computers. But things have changed. Today, we can read about it not only in the business parts of daily websites and financial newspapers, but even on the main page of such media. Bitcoin and other cryptocurrencies are becoming the subject of whole sections of news outlets. Lawmakers and regulators in jurisdictions across the globe are scrambling to put laws and rules in place that would enable or make it simpler for businesses to conduct initial coin offerings (ICOs) or token issuances. Is the word "cryptocurrency" really the most appropriate one to use? Shouldn't it be "digital money" instead? What exactly is "virtual currency"? As a result, the question we must now ask ourselves is: does cryptocurrency, or whatever we choose to name it, truly deserve this kind of attention? Is it really necessary to be so concerned?

What will be the long-term ramifications of cryptocurrency? In essence, bitcoin is entirely decentralized, which is exactly what blockchain-based services are intended to be. Because it is a financial-based blockchain, it is not overseen by any central bank or monetary body, as is the case with Bitcoin. A peer-to-peer community computer network, made up of users' computers, or "nodes," is in charge of keeping it running instead. If you are familiar with the BitTorrent protocol, the same premise applies. It is basically a digital database – referred to as a "distributed public ledger" – that is maintained via the use of encryption. Bitcoin and other cryptocurrencies are safe because they have been digitally validated via a process known as "mining." In Bitcoin mining, every information entering the Bitcoin blockchain is mathematically validated using a highly complicated digital code that has been put up on the network, which is known as a hash function. The blockchain network will check and verify any new entries into the ledger, as well as any modifications to the ledger, before they are published.

It is important to note that, although it is essentially anonymous, the mathematics underpinning it creates a worldwide public transaction log, which means that every transaction can be tracked back to its source using encryption. Without getting into too much detail, although Ethereum is quite similar to Bitcoin, its applications go beyond the purely financial aspects of things, such as mining, and include the provision of services on its own specific blockchain, which is unique to Ethereum. Among the features of Ethereum are built-in software programming languages, which may be used to build, for example, smart contracts that can be used for a variety of purposes, including the transfer and mining of the cryptocurrency's own tradeable digital token, Ether (which is even more complex than Bitcoin).

A practice known as "mooning" took place in the cryptocurrency industry just before Christmas in 2017. That means, coin prices had skyrocketed to a breathtaking level, and for many it had turned out to be the very worst moment to invest in cryptocurrencies. Because, just before Christmas, the whole market went into a meltdown, losing roughly 20% of its entire worldwide market capitalization. After that, it began to rise for a short period, which made it appear as if the crash is over. Then, in mid-January, cryptocurrency exchanges saw another meltdown, with the price of Ethereum, for example, plunging by nearly 25 percent. Here are some headlines: "Regulatory agencies are issuing 'buyer beware' warnings (certainly needed, but also because many central regulators struggle with the notion of regulating a decentralized technology). It is very speculative to invest in initial coin offers (ICO's) and cryptocurrencies, and you might potentially lose all of your money if you do so. You can, in fact, do so."

Of course, one might argue that the public stock market is risky as well (Have you heard of Lehman Brothers?), but there is little doubt that cryptocurrency exchanges are significantly more volatile than stock exchanges. However, cryptocurrency is significant and will not go away, nor will it be restricted to 100 years as some have speculated: transactions are rapid, digital, safe, and can be carried out anywhere in the globe, which in turn allows for the preservation of records without the fear of data theft. Fraud is really reduced to a minimum. To add another point of clarification, digital currencies with limited supply such as Bitcoin should not cause inflation. Because the total number of bitcoins that may ever be mined is restricted to about 21 million, there is no way for any central bank to raise the overall quantity of money in the system. Bitcoin itself is, by its very nature, limited in supply. Despite the fact that cryptocurrencies themselves are unlimited in that they may be produced by anybody, there is no evidence to support this claim. Another important point to remember in terms of significance is that, as cryptocurrencies become more widely used, it is truly the decentralized ledger technology, or blockchain, on which they are built, that has emerged as the genuine masterpiece.

Blockchain is only a platform, and the technology behind it enables cryptocurrencies and their digital tokens to function inside its confines, as previously said. The usage of blockchain may be used to almost any transaction that can be recorded. Medical records, immigration information, birth certificates, insurance policies, and other types of data can all be saved and guaranteed using blockchain technology. The implementation of smart contracts based on the Ethereum blockchain - protocols that enable contracts to be self-executed whenever certain circumstances are satisfied - will also ultimately make headlines as a result of their widespread adoption. It is important to remember that cryptocurrency is a very new kind of money, having only been around for around 10 years at the most.

The ability to leave the "keys" to your coins in your account when you purchase digital currency on a trading platform, or exchange, is one kind of storage that you may have when you purchase digital currency on a trading platform, or exchange. However, you may also take them away from the platform to a personal cryptocurrency wallet, which can either be software that is linked to the Internet (a hot wallet) or a device that is fully offline (cold storage). First and foremost, there is relatively little competition in the market at the moment. Are you shocked by this? Yes, it is correct. Yes, there is a steady increase in interest in this issue, but in general, there is still a lot of rivalry in this field. This market is still considered to be "wild" and untamed.

The reason for this is because, as we have previously indicated, the majority of people are wary of new trends and endeavors, which is understandable. Second, you may earn substantial profits in this market at the moment. Even if cryptocurrency prices are still in the early stages of growth and development, you may still make a respectable amount of money. Profits may be made as long as risks are managed prudently and in a timely manner.

Third, there are a large number of freeloaders on the market at the moment. They come to the crypto currency market in order to make a fast buck without learning anything about the issue. Typically, such individuals are recruited through pyramid schemes run by self-proclaimed "experts" who instruct others while having little or no actual knowledge of the subject matter. I must acknowledge that the market favored such individuals in the beginning, when they had a good possibility of making a lot of money at the time they did so. However, in today's world, if you want to do something similar in the crypto market, you would have to put up significant work. Fourth, there are very few hazards in the market at the moment. Five years ago, the majority of people were looking forward to the day when cryptocurrency would be legally prohibited.

Today, many nations all around the globe are beginning to acknowledge the importance of cryptocurrency as a legitimate currency. Cryptocurrency has gathered such momentum that it is impossible for anybody to simply turn the clock back. Do you honestly believe that this reality does not demonstrate that you may invest your money without fear of being subjected to a variety of bans and restrictions? Lastly, before going on to discuss the rules of the game in the cryptocurrency market, it is worthwhile to think about what the future of bitcoin may look like via the lens of the Tesla company. Tesla's current price is expected to be so high that, according to expert predictions, it will be unable to recoup its costs for at least 300 years after purchase. Why, therefore, do clever experts place such a high value on Tesla's products? Let's see if we can figure things out.

These days, an electric automobile is gorgeous and fashionable, but it is also pricey and not very useful as a mode of transportation. Experts, on the other hand, are not anxious about today because they see a world that may become a reality in 20 or 30 years. You may visualize your old, beloved automobile in the future, but experts think of some type of emission free semi-flying vehicle or even something much more advanced than that. The electric car, as a result, will have a long and prosperous future, and Tesla is expected to have a dominant position in the industry. It turns out that, for the most part, no one can predict whether Tesla will be able to maintain its dominant position in the market for the next 20-30 years. Many individuals, on the other hand, are certain that it will, and this conviction leads them to invest in the firm. What is the relationship between this example and the future of cryptocurrency? The cryptocurrency (as well as the electric car) is now considered meaningless by some, while others see it as a stylish, intriguing, and technically curious fad. Nonetheless, there is a tendency. However, this little drop of water now has the potential to expand into a vast dominate sea in the near future.

Opportunities in Cryptocurrency

For anybody who is new to investing (in anything) or is a seasoned investor who has only had exposure to other types of financial assets other than cryptocurrencies, the question of why you should consider adding cryptocurrencies in your portfolio is undoubtedly on their mind. You've most likely heard a little bit about Bitcoin here and there throughout the years. Other cryptocurrencies such as Ethereum and Dogecoin may even be familiar to you by now. And then, what exactly is the big deal about all these amusing-sounding coins in the first place? Has anybody considered Litecoin to be nothing more than a very light currency that will not take up much room in your physical wallet?

'Is a Bitcoin constructed from scraps and fragments of other precious coins?' you may wonder. In the first place, why would you want to put money into a collection of pennies? There are a rising number of reasons why cryptocurrency trading may be beneficial to many investors. These range from the basic act of diversification to the more thrilling act of participating in the revolution that is changing how we see money. Throughout this chapter, I will demonstrate some of the most exciting characteristics of this brand-new investment phenomenon. "Don't put all your eggs in one basket," as the saying goes, describes diversification.

Literally everything in life may be improved by following this recommendation. Do not pack all of your clothes in your checked-in baggage while you are travelling. In case your baggage is misplaced, pack an extra pair of underpants and a shirt in your carry-on. As a former frequent flyer, trust me on this one. There are several approaches that may be used to achieve financial diversification. Various financial assets, such as stocks, bonds, foreign currency (FX), and other similar instruments, may be used to diversify your investment portfolio. Technology, healthcare, and entertainment are examples of industries in which you may diversify through stocks. With the right investing time horizons (mid- and long-term), you can better manage your investment money. Including several promising cryptocurrencies in your investing portfolios is a great benefit since they will help to balance out your portfolio's overall risk.

Considering how different the cryptocurrency business is from conventional industries, diversification may boost the likelihood of optimizing the development of your portfolio's value in the future. It is possible that the cryptocurrency market would respond differently to various geopolitical and financial events, and this is one of the primary reasons for the increased potential. Here are some of the rationales behind why some businesses are already using cryptocurrency to have your corporation thinking about it: New demographic groups may be reached with cryptocurrency. Users are often members of a younger, more technologically advanced clientele that place a high importance on openness in their business dealings Recent research discovered that up to 40% of consumers who pay with cryptocurrency are first-time customers, and their purchase quantities are twice as large as those of customers who pay with credit card. This new technology may be more well-known inside your organization if you start introducing it soon. It may also assist the corporation in positioning itself in this vital growing market in preparation for a future that may incorporate central bank digital currency. Traditional assets that have been tokenized, as well as new asset classes, might provide access to fresh capital and liquidity pools via cryptography. Using cryptocurrency provides a number of advantages over traditional financial instruments.

For example, programmable money may allow real-time and precise revenue-sharing while also increasing transparency to make back-office reconciliation more straightforward and convenient. It is becoming more common for businesses to discover that critical customers and suppliers choose to conduct business with them through cryptocurrency. To ensure seamless exchanges with important stakeholders, your company may want a position that allows it to accept and distribute cryptocurrency. Using cryptocurrency, you may improve a wide range of more typical Treasury tasks, such as those listed below. Enabling money transactions that are easy to complete, real-time, and secure Assistance in enhancing the enterprise's control over its capital. Managing the risks and possibilities associated with investing in digital technology as an alternative or balancing asset to cash, which may devalue over time due to inflation, cryptocurrency may prove to be a viable option or balancing asset. In addition to being a tradable asset, cryptocurrency has done very well over the previous five years, with bitcoin, for example, outperforming the market. There are, without a doubt, significant volatility concerns to consider, which must be taken into account. When evaluating the use of cryptocurrency in your company's operations, the first question to ask yourself is: Do we want to store crypto on our balance sheet or do we want to simply use crypto-enabled payment methods? The optimal route for your company will be determined after a thorough evaluation of the many options available to achieve your goals. Consider the possible advantages, downsides, expenses, risks, system requirements, and other aspects of the project before moving forward with it. Following are some general considerations for your organization as it begins on its crypto adventure, which will be divided into two categories.

A Short History of Cryptocurrency

Wei Dai presented a description of "b-money" in 1998, which he described as an anonymous, distributed electronic currency system. Nick Szabo came up with the concept of bitGold shortly after. It was an electronic money system that required users to fulfil a proof of work function, with solutions being cryptographically compiled and published. It was similar to bitcoin and other currencies that would follow it. Hal Finney, who was inspired by the work of Dai and Szabo, eventually developed a money system based on a reusable proof of work, which was an important step towards the development of Bitcoin. Bitcoin, the world's first decentralized cryptocurrency, was founded in 2009 by an anonymous programmer known only as Satoshi Nakamoto. A cryptographic hash algorithm, SHA-256, was employed as part of the proof-of-work strategy in this case.

Numerous different currencies have been developed since then, yet only a handful have proven to be effective. There were 1574 bitcoin ATMs deployed throughout the globe by September 2017, with an average cost of 9.05 percent charged by each machine. In September 2017, an average of three bitcoin ATMs were deployed every day, according to CoinDesk.

The legal position of currencies varies significantly from nation to country, and in many cases, it is currently unclear or evolving. While some nations have openly permitted their use and commerce, others have prohibited or severely limited their use and sale. Similarly, different government organizations, departments, and courts have assigned different classifications to bitcoins. Early in 2014, the Chinese Central Bank prohibited financial institutions from dealing with bitcoins because of the country's unusually rapid adoption of the cryptocurrency. It is unlawful to buy products in Russia using any money other than the Russian ruble, despite the fact that other currencies are legal in the country. The Internal Revenue Service (IRS) of the United States of America (USA) declared on March 25, 2014, that bitcoin would be considered as property, rather than cash, for tax purposes. Because of this, bitcoin will be liable to capital gains tax. The advantage of this decision is a clarification of the legality of bitcoin. Investors no longer have to be concerned about whether or not their bitcoin investments or profits are unlawful, or about how to disclose them to the Internal Revenue Service. A report released by scholars from Oxford and Warwick demonstrated that bitcoin exhibits several features that are more similar to the precious metals market than conventional currencies, and so is in accord with the IRS judgement, even though the reasons for the decision are different.

For some currencies, there have been legal difficulties that have nothing to do with governments. Coinye, for example, is an altcoin that, without permission, utilized the image of musician Kanye West as its logo. When Kanye West's lawyers learned about the publication of Coinye, previously known as Coinye West, they immediately wrote a stop and desist letter. It said that Coinye was engaging in intentional trademark infringement, unfair competition, cyberpiracy, and dilution, and ordered Coinye to cease and desist from utilizing Kanye West's image and name in any manner. Since the introduction of bitcoin in 2009, the popularity and demand for online currencies have grown exponentially, raising fears that the uncontrolled person-to-person global commerce that currencies enable would pose a danger to civilization. There is widespread concern that cryptocurrencies will be used as tools by anonymous cyber criminals. Because of their marked lack of regulation, cryptocurrency networks have drawn the attention of many users seeking decentralized exchange and use of currency; however, this same lack of regulation has been criticized as potentially providing an opportunity for criminals seeking to evade taxes and launder money to use cryptocurrency networks. Transactions that take place via the usage and exchange of these alternative currencies are not tied to traditional banking institutions, which might make tax evasion easier for individuals.

It becomes exceedingly difficult to account for transactions performed using current currencies, which is a mechanism of exchange that is complicated and (in some circumstances) impossible to trace since the revenue service bases its calculations on what a receiver reports to the government. The anonymity systems that most currencies provide may potentially be used to launder money in a more straightforward manner. Rather than laundering money via a complex web of financial players and offshore bank accounts, laundering money with altcoins may be accomplished anonymously through trades on a decentralized exchange.

On August 6, 2013, Magistrate Judge Amos Mazzant of the United States District Court for the Eastern District of Texas ruled that cryptocurrency (expressly bitcoin) is a currency or form of money because it can be used as money (it can be used to purchase goods and services, pay for individual living expenses, and be exchanged for conventional currencies). Following this decision, the Securities and Exchange Commission (SEC) gained authority over claims of securities fraud utilizing Bitcoin.

On October 26, 2013, GBL, a Chinese bitcoin trading site, was forced to close its doors without warning. Subscribers who were unable to log in suffered losses of up to $5 million in bitcoin. The collapse of Mt. Gox, the world's biggest bitcoin exchange, generated worldwide news in February 2014, prompting many to question the legitimacy of cryptocurrencies. The organization reported that it had lost roughly $473 million in bitcoins belonging to its customers, most likely as a result of theft. This was the equivalent of around 750,000 bitcoins, or nearly 7% of the total number of bitcoins in circulation. The price of bitcoin went from a peak of around $1,160 in December to a low of less than $400 in February, among other reasons, as a result of the crisis. A federal investigation into Silk Road, an underground illicit black market that federal prosecutors shut down in 2013, led to the indictment of two now-former agents from the Drug Enforcement Administration and the United States Secret Service on March 31, 2015.

This implies that their addresses, as well as customer evaluations and open forums referring to the medications already on the market, may all be located without implicating any particular kind of user. It is because of this kind of anonymity that users on both sides of black marketplaces are able to avoid the reach of law enforcement. As a consequence, law enforcement continues to pursue a policy of single-outing particular markets and drug traffickers in order to reduce the supply of illegal drugs. While law enforcement is unable to keep up with the quickly developing and anonymous marketplaces of dark markets, dealers and suppliers are able to remain one step ahead of the authorities.

An Initial Coin Offering (ICO) is a method of raising capital for a new cryptocurrency enterprise that is not governed by any government. An initial coin offering (ICO) is a method for entrepreneurs to circumvent the laborious and regulated capital-raising procedures that are required by venture capitalists or banks. When a cryptocurrency project launches an ICO campaign, a share of the cryptocurrency is offered to early supporters of the project in return for legal cash or other currencies, most often Bitcoin or Ethereum. There are a variety of timestamping systems used by cryptocurrencies to circumvent the necessity for a trusted third party to timestamp transactions that are uploaded to the blockchain ledger.

Bitcoin and the Modern Cryptocurrency Boom

Blockchain-based record-keeping, built-in scarcity, and decentralized control distinguish Bitcoin as the first modern cryptocurrency. Bitcoin is widely regarded as the first publicly used means of exchange to combine decentralized control, user anonymity, record-keeping via a blockchain, and built-in scarcity. In a 2008 white paper produced by Satoshi Nakamoto, a pseudonymous individual or group, the concept of bitcoin was initially articulated. In early 2009, Satoshi Nakamoto made Bitcoin available to the general public, and a small number of passionate enthusiasts immediately started trading and mining the cryptocurrency.

Several comparable cryptocurrencies, including popular alternatives like as Litecoin, started to develop by the end of 2010, the first of what would ultimately be hundreds of such currencies. Around the same time period, the first public Bitcoin exchanges were established. WordPress became the first large business to accept Bitcoin payments when it began accepting them in late 2012. Others, like online electronics shop Newegg.com, Expedia, Microsoft, and Tesla, joined the party later in the year. Hundreds of thousands of shops now accept bitcoin as a valid payment option, making it the world's most popular cryptocurrency.

Despite the fact that few cryptocurrencies other than Bitcoin are generally accepted for merchant payments, a rising number of active exchanges enable holders to trade their cryptocurrencies for Bitcoin or fiat currencies, hence offering vital liquidity and flexibility. In addition, since the late 2010s, large business and institutional investors have been keeping a careful eye on what they refer to as the "crypto area." Though its development is under wraps, Facebook's Libra project may prove to be the first viable cryptocurrency alternative to fiat currencies, its growing pains show that complete parity with fiat currencies is still years away.

Blockchain & Defi Explained

Before starting to dive in deeper, it is critical to grasp the challenges that Blockchain technology seeks to answer, before delving into the technical specifics of the blockchain technology itself. The Blockchain is a revolutionary technology, but what exactly can it achieve that our existing technology cannot? A fundamental problem in the way humans think about transactions, trust, and social institutions was identified by Bitcoin and Blockchain technology's early users as a source of contention. In the United States, the early versions of Blockchain were developed at the same time as the 2007 financial crisis, during which many individuals lost trust in the institutions of society that were meant to look out for the interests of the average man and woman.

As a result of the financial crisis, individuals lost trust in the banking system, but they also lost faith in the government's ability to control financial markets and in the media's ability to uncover impending problems. It is generally agreed upon that our institutions have weaknesses and are not ideal answers in every circumstance. They do, however, provide solutions to trust-related issues, and they have been doing so for centuries. It's very possible that we're now experiencing the most tranquil and pleasant period in human history. The benefits and strengths of any alternative to our present institutions must be clearly defined.

The concept behind Blockchain is to replace institutions operated by fallible human beings with technology that is both more efficient and more empowering for people to do their tasks. Creating a system that allows strangers to trust one another without the need for a bank or a government as an intermediary would help to alleviate one of society's most intractable stumbling blocks, experts say. You'd need a strong method for reaching agreement among strangers in order to do so, and the Blockchain's developers think that power rests in decentralization rather than in centralized systems. Virtually all blockchain (and other cryptographic) applications are founded on the principle of decentralization, which is at the heart of the technology.

Instead of a strict, sluggish central authority making choices and controlling interactions, Blockchain aspires to deliver regulatory power back to the people who are affected by the decisions and connections. Instead of putting faith in a big organization, Blockchain fosters confidence by establishing agreement among participants. Although the Blockchain technology may be unfamiliar to some readers, experts believe that it has the potential to usher in a period of significant change in the world of technological innovation. As a result, a number of businesses are looking for lucrative prospects in the sector of Blockchain Applications Development. Because blockchain technology is still in its early stages, the majority of the population is unaware of this recent development in technology. If you are one of those who want to have a thorough understanding of technology, just continue reading the information given below.

Transactions are recorded in a digital ledger, with Bitcoin or other cryptocurrencies serving as the medium of exchange. According to Blockchain specialists, this technology enables a very secure means of documenting or executing all transactions, agreements, and contracts in a single location. Aside from that, Blockchain is useful for anything that requires verification and storage in a secure digital environment. From the very beginning of the network, the database is shared among a large number of users who are all granted access to the information pertaining to all of the transactions in the database. The entire size of the network changes depending on the number of members, which may range from two or three to hundreds of users.

As a result, specialists are attempting to apply it to a variety of goals, with Bitcoin serving as the most visible and prominent use of the technology at the present time. People who participate in financial transactions have benefited from Bitcoin since it was first introduced back in 2008. Aside from that, the specialists are looking at methods in which the same technology may be utilized to resolve or lessen difficulties related to safety, conflict resolution, or religious belief. When a new transaction is made, a specialized computer programmed is utilized to create the blockchain, which then automatically updates the information in the database. Unlike traditional databases, blockchains store blocks of transactions that have been hashed or encoded.

Blockchains are formed when a code is combined with the hash of the block that came before it to create a chain. For the overall security of the database, it is necessary to validate each block in this procedure.

As previously said, the Blockchain is attempting to make technology more beneficial for those who want an irrefutable record of transactions to be maintained. Blockchain technology delivers the highest level of clarity and openness, and it has the potential to be a powerful instrument in the fight against corruption and other criminal activity. Due to the use of Blockchain technology, all transactions take place in a secure environment in which all of the information are encrypted with the production of a unique transaction number, which is then entered in the ledger as a placeholder number. As a result, the transaction's details would not be visible to all of the users in this scenario. The transaction will, however, be noticed by the network. Due to the fact that the person with malicious designs must access every computer on the network in order to make modifications to the database, any change in a scam is severely restricted. As the relevance of Blockchain development grows, a rising number of people and companies are seeking for a trustworthy and dependable Blockchain Development Company.

Blockchain is an unquestionably helpful creation that is bringing about an unstoppable change in the worldwide commercial industry. As a result of its progress, not only have companies benefited, but so have those who have benefited from it. Their operational actions have not been clearly defined since its public disclosure to the globe. The most often asked question is, "What is Blockchain?" This is the most frequently asked question. To begin with, blockchain technology functions as a platform that permits the transfer of digital information without the danger of it being duplicated by other parties. The basis for a strong backbone of a new form of online space has been built, in a sense, by this event.

Originating as a way to educate the general public about Bitcoin - specifically, how to explain to non-technical people about the functions of its algorithms, hash functions, and digital signature property - today's technology enthusiasts are discovering new and innovative ways to put this remarkable invention to use in order to usher in an entirely new way of doing business around the world. Defining blockchain as a whole, it is a kind of algorithm and data distribution system that allows for electronic currency to be managed without the need for interference from a centralized administration, and it is designed to record all financial transactions as well as anything else of value. Distributed ledger technology (also known as blockchain technology) is a kind of technology that was first developed to support the Bitcoin cryptocurrency.

However, after widespread condemnation and rejection, the technology was altered to be used in more productive applications. Think of a spreadsheet that has been practically supplemented hundreds of thousands of times over a wide range of computer devices to provide a clear image. Consider the possibility that these networks are meant to periodically update this spreadsheet. Exactly this is what the blockchain technology is all about. In the blockchain, information is maintained in the form of a shared sheet, the data of which is reconciled on a regular schedule.

A realistic approach that has a long list of unmistakable advantages in the first place, the blockchain data does not reside in a single, centralized repository. This implies that anything that is kept there is available for public inspection and validation. There is also no centralized information storage platform that hackers might use to damage the data stored there. A million computers are literally connected to it at the same time, and its data may be viewed by anybody having an internet connection to access it. Blockchain technology is something that helps to reduce the amount of internet space available for use by computers. The look is sophisticated while being grounded in the environment. Blocks of valid information are kept on the blockchain platform, which is equally viewable on all networks, in a manner similar to providing material to the broader public via the World Wide Web.

To be clear, the blockchain cannot be controlled by a single person, company, or identity, and there is no single point of failure in its operation. As blockchain continues to evolve, it will serve as a legitimate, dependable worldwide stage for commercial transactions, similar to how the internet has established itself over the previous 30 years to be a dependable medium for communication. Legendary industry figures have said that the blockchain operates on a subconscious level of mind. Every now and again, it does a virtual self-check.

A self-auditing technology, it reconciles every transaction, known as a block, that takes place onboard at regular intervals, just as a self-auditing system does. Two important characteristics of blockchain are born as a result of this: it is incredibly transparent while also being impenetrable to corruption. All transactions carried out on this server are integrated into the network, making the whole process very transparent to the general public at all times, regardless of when they take place. Apart from that, it takes a tremendous amount of time and computer power to alter or remove information from a blockchain transaction. Frauds can be readily distinguished in this environment. As a result, it has earned the title "incorruptible." No specific law or regulation exists regarding who should or may make advantage of this incredible technological advancement. While banks, business giants, and global economies are the most likely consumers of the technology at this time, it may be used for everyday transactions by the common population in the future. In terms of disadvantages, blockchain only has one: universal adoption.

How Does the Blockchain Work?

A public ledger and encryption are used together to establish trust between participants while still safeguarding their anonymity, which is the most basic definition of Blockchain. Getting our heads around the technicalities of how this works is a little more challenging, but we'll need to do so in order to truly appreciate the brilliance that lies at the heart of Blockchain technology. While Blockchain technology may encompass a wide range of features, the principles of the technology are included in the name of the technology: Blockchain. The block: A block is a collection of transactions that occurred during a certain period of time. It comprises all of the information that has been processed across the network in the last several minutes. At any one moment, the network can only construct one block. The chain is comprised of individual blocks that are connected to one another using cryptographic techniques.

Despite the fact that these algorithms are challenging for computers to calculate, they often take several minutes to solve even the fastest computers on the planet. Once the problem is solved, the cryptographic chain secures the block in place, making it impossible to modify. More on this in a moment, but for now, let's just take a quick look at it. The length of the chain increases as time goes on. As soon as a new block is formed, all participating computers on the network collaborate to validate the transactions contained inside the block and protect the block's position within the chain. It is the ledger that serves as the most essential component of the Blockchain. In this location, information about the accounts on the network is kept safe and secure. The ledger included inside the Blockchain is what takes the place of the ledger found in a bank or other financial institution. This ledger is often comprised of account numbers, transactions, and balances in the case of a cryptocurrency. Every time you submit a transaction to the Blockchain, you're adding information to the ledger regarding where the money is coming from and where it's going. A Blockchain ledger is a digital record that is disseminated across the network. Everyone on the network maintains their own copy of the ledger, which is updated whenever a new transaction is sent to the network. Blockchain promises to replace banks and other financial institutions via the use of a "shared ledger."

Instead of having the bank maintain a single official copy of the ledger, everyone will maintain their own copy of the ledger, and we will then validate transactions by reaching an agreement on the final version. Each Blockchain system has its own ledger, and the various ledgers operate in a variety of ways (as we'll see in a moment). The next notion is one that is tough to grasp: there is no such thing as a Bitcoin in the real world. Of course, there are no actual Bitcoins to be found. That's something you were probably already aware of. However, there are no Bitcoins stored on a computer's hard disc or anywhere else.

To identify a Bitcoin, you cannot point to a physical thing, digital file or piece of code and say, "This is what it looks like. As opposed to this, the whole Bitcoin network is nothing more than a collection of transaction records. Every transaction in the history of Bitcoin is recorded on the Bitcoin Blockchain, which serves as a distributed ledger for all transactions. If you wish to demonstrate that you have 20 Bitcoins, the only method to do so is to provide links to the transactions in which you obtained those 20 Bitcoins. This is a trait shared by almost all blockchain technologies. The currency is represented by the transaction history. There isn't any distinction between the two. To enable better anonymity and privacy in transactions, several new cryptocurrencies are modifying the way their ledgers are maintained. When sending and receiving transactions, they employ identity masking methods to conceal who sent and who received the transaction while still preserving the functionality of the distributed ledger. A block's ledger is its central component; however, it is not the only component that goes into a freshly generated block. Every block must have a header and a footer, which are both essential.

Crypto Mining & Cloud Mining

Cryptocurrency mining, in a nutshell, is a word that refers to the act of collecting cryptocurrency as a reward for work that you have completed. Who does crypto mining, and why? Some are seeking for a second source of income to supplement their current one. Increasing financial independence without the interference of governments or banks is important to others.

The term "mine" was chosen specifically to refer to the process of gold mining. Cryptocurrency mining or Bitcoin mining is the process of creating new cryptocurrencies or Bitcoins. Those who own or operate mining machines are referred to as miners. The word "miner" is often used to refer to the computational hardware that is required to locate Bitcoin (or another cryptocurrency) in a network of computers. The process of mining involves determining the digital signature of a block. An array of data containing information on transactions that have occurred on the Bitcoin network since the previous block was formed is known as a block in the Bitcoin network. A bitcoin reward is given to a network member who successfully deciphers the digital signature algorithm. The same time, in order to get a "gold bar" in the form of a precious-generating transaction, a miner must filter through masses of "dead rock," which is comprised of hashes that are ineligible for inclusion in the block. Each new block has a digital signature that is generated based on the preceding block, as shown in the diagram below.

The blocks cling to one another and combine to create a chain of blocks known as the Blockchain network. The majority of people believe that mining is a source of money produced from an electrical outlet. However, in reality, it is a fantastic piece of meticulous labor that has been rewarded with money by the system itself. The creation of new currencies is a time-consuming and costly procedure, despite the fact that both the client code and the bitcoin protocol code are completely open. For example, you are not permitted to create more bitcoins than the amount originally anticipated by the technology's originator. To get fresh coins, you must make significant expenditures in equipment, facilities, cooling systems, power, and other resources. That is why Bitcoin is referred to as "digital gold" and is portrayed in the form of gold coins on the Bitcoin blockchain.

Cloud Mining

A cloud mining operation is a kind of cryptocurrency mining that makes use of a distant data center with pooled computing capacity in order to mine cryptocurrency coins. It is possible to mine Bitcoins or other cryptocurrencies with this kind of mining without having to manage hardware. An underground facility owned by the mining firm is utilized to store the mining rigs. For mining contracts, the client must first register. It is via cloud mining that the most recent Bitcoins are added to the public ledger. You may make money without having to put any money into it if you use cloud mining services. However, in order to set up a mining rig, you will either an Application-Specific Integrated Circuit (ASIC) or a graphics processing unit (GPU).

Adding individual blocks to the Blockchain is the purpose of a miner in a cloud mining network, which is achieved by solving complicated mathematical problems. There will be a significant amount of computational and electrical power required for this. While several miners compete to add each block to the Blockchain, the miner who solves the puzzle will be the one who adds the block to the Blockchain, along with all of the transactions that have been allowed by the blockchain's administrators. As a result, this miner gets credited with the reward.

ICO (Initial Coin Offering)

ICO stands for initial coin offering, and it is the technique for generating cash for cryptocurrency-related businesses. It is mostly utilized by startups as a means of circumventing the regulated capital-raising procedures employed by banks or venture capitalists, and it is becoming more popular. One such cryptocurrency initiative is Ether, which has already received a significant amount of money via an initial coin offering (ICO). When a company goes public, this investment strategy is quite similar to the Initial Public Offering (IPO), in which interested investors buy shares of the company. During an initial coin offering (ICO), the coins produced are referred to as tokens, and they may be compared to the shares of a corporation offered to investors. So far, initial coin offerings (ICOs) have dominated the blockchain industry, and many people consider them unregulated securities. This may make it possible for the entrepreneurs to obtain the funds necessary to launch a particular cryptocurrency enterprise. Basically, this is a shortcut that eliminates many of the hassles prevalent in the venture capital process.

A certain amount of a cryptocurrency is sold to the project's early backers in return for legal money or another cryptocurrency, such as Bitcoin, in every initial coin offering (ICO). To be successful, every cryptocurrency startup must develop a detailed plan in its white paper that outlines the project's goals, the problems the project will solve after its completion, the amount of money required to fund the venture, as well as the percentage of the coin that will be retained by the project's founders should the venture be successful. If the enterprise fails, the money is refunded to the investors, and the initial coin offering (ICO) is deemed a failure. The project is either started or completed if the finances are sufficient. If the funds are insufficient, the project is terminated. Overall, initial coin offerings (ICOs) are simple to arrange with the help of technologies such as ERC20 Token Standards, which streamline the process of generating any cryptographic assets. In exchange for their money in the form of Ether or Bitcoin, investors make contributions to the ICO development by submitting their funds to a pre-determined smart contract, which may hold their funds and eventually distribute the equal value of the new token to the investors.

Participation in an initial coin offering (ICO) is open to anybody since there are few, if any, limitations on this initiative, given that the token is not considered a financial instrument. With initial coin offerings (ICOs), one may quickly earn stratospheric profits in comparison to the worldwide pool in which many investors find themselves. Nonetheless, there is a significant margin of danger since they are very speculative in nature, as the majority of them seek money prior to the launch of the product.

How ICOs Work

It is possible to think of an initial coin offering as a sophisticated form of crowdfunding that has arisen outside of the traditional banking system. Crowdfunding has allowed businesses to embark on some very remarkable undertakings, and they have successfully raised the funds necessary to complete their endeavors using this method. The initial coin offering (ICO) may be thought of as the cryptocurrency equivalent of crowdfunding.

This concept has been well-integrated into the crypto industry, and it is here to stay. In an initial coin offering (ICO), which may last up to one or more weeks, anybody is always welcome to purchase new tokens in exchange for Bitcoin or any other existing cryptocurrency. Every initial coin offering (ICO) has a specific limit or goal for project funding, which means that every single token always has a pre-determined price that does not change throughout the duration of the initial coin offering; this is what keeps the token supply static throughout the duration of the initial coin offering. It is also possible to have a static supply with a dynamic financing aim, in which case the distribution of the token will be dependent on the amount of money collected, resulting in a greater token price if the project obtains more funding. Pre-ICO sales, as the name implies, provide investors with an opportunity to purchase tokens prior to the start of the official sales.

A pre-ICO sale is based on a smart contract, which allows the cash to be kept separate from the main sale in order to prevent misunderstanding during the official sale. In most cases, just a small amount of money is raised during the presale stage since the ICO tokens are sold at a discounted price during this time, in addition to specific benefits being offered to the investors. Pre-sale activities are initiated by various groups for a variety of reasons. As an example, below are some of the most often cited reasons why corporations commence presales ahead to the formal launch of a crowdsourcing campaign. Most businesses use it as a promotional technique to increase their sales. An initial coin offering (ICO) is usually a convenient technique of dispersing funds and assuring that investors would support the forthcoming enterprise. An ICO presale is more of a "buy one, get one free" kind of approach, as opposed to a traditional ICO.

As a result of the presale, more people are becoming aware of the ICO. An ICO is usually the greatest time to invest since the tokens are offered at a reduced price because the companies provide incentives that will grab the attention of investors. Following the completion of the project and the acquisition of a sufficient number of long-term investors, the firms see a rise in their profitability. A presale in an ICO is often held with the primary goal of attracting angel investors who will support the company's operating expenditures while the company's white papers and roadmaps are being finalized and developed. While an initial coin offering (ICO) presale is a fantastic method for a business to collect capital to help it get off the ground, it may also be detrimental to the firm, particularly if a large number of tokens are sold at a cheap price during the offer time. A month or so before the formal launch of the initial coin offering (ICO), most firms begin their presale period. However, this is not an opportunity that can be made accessible to everyone since the presale may be accompanied by certain restrictions. A KYC (know your customer) permission and, secondly, the ability to contribute the minimum amount are required in order to participate in this.

However, all of this is only true for legitimate companies. It is difficult to determine which ICOs are legitimate and which ones are not, so it is best not to try your luck if you do not know what you are doing. An initial coin offering (ICO) presale can be extremely profitable for investors who act fast enough or have insider information about an upcoming project, but it is also rife with scam artists. So, be careful when you invest in ICOs.

Different Types of Cryptocurrencies

Many people believe that the words "coin," and "token," which are frequently used as synonymous, are interchangeable. However, they represent two distinct ideas. So, why do so many crypto traders mix coins and tokens up, and what is the key difference between them?

In a rapidly changing sector of cryptocurrency, new words are being created at an exponential rate, which has resulted in misunderstanding and misuse of them. Despite the fact that many of them aren't currently circulating as money and were never intended to be, all coins and tokens are referred to as "cryptocurrency." According to the definition, currency is a means of exchange, unit of account, or store of value. Because Bitcoin has all of these characteristics, the term "cryptocurrency" is appropriate in this case. However, all coins and tokens, after Bitcoin's success, were dubbed "cryptocurrency" by default, despite the fact that many of them do not fulfill required criteria. As a result, coins and tokens are both referred to as "cryptocurrency." This situation is deceptive to would-be purchasers who want to buy cryptocurrencies but wind up being the owners of tokens. The majority of cryptocurrency users, own both coins and tokens.

To ensure that you understand what you're saying the next time you make a reference to tokens or coins, let us go over some of the most major contrasts between the two. Also, I will present you with some explanations of how they are used.

Coins

Coins are digital money created with encryption technology that preserve their value over time and are sometimes referred to as altcoins or alternate cryptocurrency coins. It's essentially a digital replica of currency. Bitcoin was the first cryptocurrency, and it established the bar for what it means to be a cryptocurrency. Crypto coins and tokens are both similar to real-world money in that they exhibit certain characteristics.

A coin is defined by operating on its own blockchain. A blockchain keeps track of all transactions that involve its native crypto coin. When you pay someone with Ethereum, the receipt goes to the Ethereum blockchain. If the same person pays you back later with Bitcoin, the receipt goes to the Bitcoin blockchain. Each transaction is protected by encryption and is accessible by any member of the network.

A currency is defined by its own blockchain, which serves as the foundation for all transactions. All transactions carried out using the native cryptocurrency are recorded on the blockchain. The Ethereum transaction receipt resides on the Ethereum blockchain if you pay someone with Ether. If you repay someone later with Bitcoin, the transaction is recorded on the Bitcoin blockchain. Every trade is secured by encryption and may be viewed by any network member.

A coin is also used as money. Bitcoin was created solely with the intention of replacing traditional currency. The desire for transparency or anonymity drove the development of a wide range of other currencies. You may now pay for items and services from a variety of major businesses with cryptocurrency coins. Bitcoin has been recognized by the government of El Salvador as a legal tender in addition to the US dollar.

A coin can be mined. You can make money by mining Bitcoin on the Proof of Work method. Bitcoin hunters use this approach to increase their profits. The issue with this is that there aren't many more Bitcoins to be mined, which means the process gets more difficult every day. The alternative approach is Proof of Stake (PoS), which is a more modern method of obtaining coins. It consumes less energy and is simpler to execute. Cardano is one of the most popular cryptocurrencies that use this technology.

Tokens

Tokens do not have their own blockchain, like bitcoin. They execute on the blockchains of other cryptocurrencies, such as Ethereum, instead of having their own. Smart contracts are used in the trade and payments between users when crypto currency transactions are handled by blockchain. They're basically a set of rules that allow for transactions or payments to be made between people.

Tokens are digital assets produced by the project that may be utilized as a means of payment in the ecosystem, carrying out similar duties to coins but with one significant distinction: it also confers rights on the owner to participate in the network. It may be used for a variety of purposes, including digital asset, representing a company's share, giving access to the project's functionalities, and more. New projects tend to explore formerly unknown aspects of tokens' capabilities. Utility and security tokens are the two different types. Security tokens represent an asset or a service, whereas utility tokens represent a use case inside the project.

Creating a token is simpler than creating a coin since you don't need to create a new code or modify an existing one. You simply utilize a standard template from platforms like Ethereum, which are blockchain-based and enable anybody to issue tokens in only a few easy steps. Using a template to generate tokens allows for seamless interoperability, allowing users to store various kinds of tokens in one wallet. Ethereum was the first to make token creation easier, and it has been a major reason for the fast-growing number of crypto projects.

When a token is used, it physically moves from one location to another. The trading of NFTs (non-fungible tokens) is a great illustration of this. They are unique items, so any change in ownership must be recorded individually. In many cases, NFTs have little to no actual economic value and are simply used for decoration or sentiment. In a certain way, they're comparable to utility tokens but you can't compel any services using them. It differs from coins in that crypto coins do not move; only account balances are updated. When you send money from one person to another, it doesn't disappear. The bank adjusted both accounts' balances as well as the fees, which is the same thing that occurs with blockchain. Simply stated, a token represents what you possess, while a coin indicates what you can own.

Stablecoins

Even though it seems to be a contradiction, in the whole wild and woolly world of cryptocurrencies, some of the world's top financial authorities are most concerned about the type of digital money that is meant to be the safest: stablecoins. Even the term conveys a sense of security and dependability. The usage of stablecoins in general, and in particular the largest stablecoins by market capitalization, Tether, has come under increased attention amid concerns that they might represent a danger to cryptocurrency users and potentially the entire financial system. Concerning Tether, there's also the matter of whether the $69 billion in safe assets that the corporation that issued the currency claims to be backing it are, in fact, secure assets.

Stablecoins are digital assets that are sometimes referred to as coins and other times as tokens, and which are intended to maintain their value over time. That is, to experience just the type of volatility that may be seen in conventional currencies, which have price fluctuations that are often far lower than those experienced by Bitcoin. There are two possible outcomes. Stablecoins that are tied to another asset, such as the U.S. dollar, and whose issuers claim to back up the value of their currency by hanging on to that asset or something else as secure are known as collateralized stablecoins. Some coins use algorithms to control supply and demand, ensuring that the amount of currency in circulation matches the amount of coin kept in reserve. The number of stablecoins now in circulation has reached dozens and more are on the way. Stablecoins have the potential to serve as a link between two realms that were not intended to be mixed in the first place — cryptocurrencies and conventional banking.

Thus, they may be used to protect profits from cryptocurrency trading or as a safe haven for investors who believe a slump is on the horizon. They also make it simpler to transfer payments to cryptocurrency exchanges. A large number of cryptocurrency exchanges do not have the banking links necessary to handle traditional currency deposits or withdrawals, but they may and do accept stablecoins. Stablecoins have the potential to simplify, accelerate, and lower the cost of transactions and money transfers by relying on a separate technology, known as blockchain, rather than the existing payments infrastructure. Lastly, if users are unsure about the buying power of the currency tomorrow, they will hold off on adopting it. In an ideal world, a cryptocurrency coin would preserve its buying value while experiencing the least amount of inflation feasible, which would be sufficient to incentivize people to use their tokens rather than save them.

Altcoins

The term Altcoins refers to all cryptocurrencies other than Bitcoin, even though you can argue that Ethereum does not fall into this category as well. They have certain traits in common with Bitcoin, but they are also distinct in other respects. For example, some cryptocurrencies utilize a different consensus process to generate blocks and verify transactions than others. In other words, they separate themselves from Bitcoin by offering unique or extra features, such as smart contracts or minimal price fluctuation, that Bitcoin does not. As of October 2021, there are more than 12,000 cryptocurrencies in circulation worldwide. According to CoinMarketCap, altcoins accounted for over 60% of the global cryptocurrency market in October 2021, with bitcoin accounting for the remaining 40%. Because they are developed from Bitcoin, the price changes of altcoins tend to follow in the footsteps of Bitcoin's trajectory.

Analysts believe that as cryptocurrency investment ecosystems mature and new markets for these currencies emerge, price movements for altcoins will become independent of Bitcoin's trading signals. The term "Altcoin" is a combination of the terms "alternative" and "coin," and it refers to any cryptocurrency that is not Bitcoin. The fundamental frameworks of Bitcoin and altcoins are quite similar. In this way, they may work as peer-to-peer systems or as a huge computer capable of processing massive volumes of data and transactions at the same time, depending on their configuration. In some cases, cryptocurrencies strive to become the next Bitcoin by establishing themselves as a low-cost mechanism of conducting digital transactions. However, there are many distinctions between Bitcoin and other cryptocurrencies. Bitcoin was one of the earliest iterations of a cryptocurrency, and its concept and design served as a model for the creation of other cryptocurrencies in the following years. Its implementation, on the other hand, has a number of flaws. In the case of Bitcoin, for example, Proof-of-Work (PoW)—the consensus technique used to build blocks—is both energy- and time-intensive. The possibilities of Bitcoin's smart contracts are similarly restricted. Following its inception in 2009, Bitcoin established itself as the first widely used implementation of Proof of Work technology in the world (PoW). PoW is also the foundation of many other cryptocurrencies, since it allows for safe, decentralized consensus to be achieved. Altcoins are designed to overcome Bitcoin's perceived restrictions in order to gain a competitive edge. Many cryptocurrencies, including Bitcoin and Ethereum, employ the Proof-of-Stake (PoS) consensus technique to reduce energy consumption and the time necessary to build blocks and confirm new transactions. Another example is the cryptocurrency ether (ETHUSD), which is the world's second-largest cryptocurrency by market capitalization and is utilized as gas (or payment for transaction expenses) in smart contracts on the Ethereum platform.

Altcoins also address some of the classic criticisms levelled towards Bitcoin. Stablecoins, for example, do not display the price volatility associated with Bitcoin, making them excellent vehicles for everyday transactions. Altcoins have built a market for themselves by establishing a clear distinction between themselves and the Bitcoin currency. As a result, they have garnered the attention of investors who consider them as viable alternatives to Bitcoin. The investors anticipate making money as cryptocurrencies gain more momentum and users, as well as their value increases. Many alternative cryptocurrencies (altcoins) are based on the fundamental framework offered by Bitcoin. In order to do this, most cryptocurrencies are peer-to-peer, need a mining process in which users solve complex issues by cracking blocks, and enable safe and affordable methods of conducting online transactions. However, even if they have many characteristics, altcoins are very different from one another.

Popular Cryptocurrencies

Cryptocurrencies are usually intended to be immune to manipulation and control by governments, yet as they have gained in popularity, this fundamental component of the business has come under scrutiny as a result. However, although some of these currencies may have certain amazing characteristics that Bitcoin does not have, none of them have yet been able to reach the same degree of security that Bitcoin's networks have achieved. The digital currencies listed below, in addition to Bitcoin, are some of the most significant in the world today.

While many of these cryptocurrencies have little to no support or trading volume, others have a devoted following of supporters and investors who have made them quite popular. The world of cryptocurrencies is constantly evolving, and the next big crypto project might be created as soon as tomorrow. In spite of the fact that Bitcoin is commonly regarded as the industry's pioneer, analysts use a variety of methodologies when analyzing tokens other than bitcoin. According to a popular practice among investors and analysts, rating coins in terms of market capitalization compared to one another is quite important. Even though we've taken this into account, there are a variety of additional reasons why a digital token may be featured on this list. A word of caution, though: It is not possible to cover each interesting coin out there in this book. There are already countless cryptocurrencies in existence and some coins have yet to mature to unfold their true potential.

Bitcoin

The currency that began it all is today considered to be one of the world's most valuable valuables. With a market capitalization reaching a trillion USD, the cryptocurrency is worth more than big corporations such as PayPal, Netflix and Coca Cola combined. We've already covered Bitcoin in detail in a previous part, so this piece will focus on Bitcoin as an investment vehicle. With the price of Bitcoin reaching astonishing heights per coin, many experts have said that holding Bitcoin is out of reach for the average investor. However, this is a position with which I disagree.

First and foremost, we must realize that cryptocurrencies are not the same as traditional equities in that they are not divisible. As a result, if you wanted to invest in Bitcoin, you didn't have to buy the whole coin. It is possible to purchase fractions of the coin, which means that even if you only have $100, you may get started in the cryptocurrency market. First and foremost, Bitcoin's status as a type of "digital gold" ensures that it remains the most valuable cryptocurrency in the world for now. It also makes Bitcoin an excellent investment to have as part of your portfolio since the price of many other currencies is connected to the price of Bitcoin. In addition, if you want to acquire any of the lesser recognized cryptocurrencies, you will have to do so by trading them for Bitcoin or Ethereum rather than purchasing them outright with fiat cash. This is another reason why Bitcoin should be included in every portfolio.

Bitcoin was the first solid cryptocurrency, and it was the first to be used as a medium of exchange. As previously stated, there is a cap on the total amount of bitcoin at 21 million Bitcoin in circulation. Bitcoin was created with the goal of being completely independent of any government or central bank. Blockchain technology is used instead, which is a decentralized public ledger that keeps a digital record of every Bitcoin transaction. Bitcoin is credited with establishing the fundamental system of cryptography and consensus (i.e., peer-to-peer) verification that serves as the basis for the majority of cryptocurrency systems today. So-called bitcoin miners use sophisticated computers to validate blocks of transactions and produce more bitcoins, a process known as proof-of-work that is both complicated and time-consuming.

The transactions are recorded in perpetuity on the blockchain, which aids in the validation and security of each bitcoin as well as the whole bitcoin network. Recently, environmentalists have expressed alarm about the massive amount of energy necessary to manufacture Bitcoin, which they believe will pollute the environment. Payments and digital transactions are made easier using Bitcoin, which is widely recognized as the world's first decentralized cryptocurrency that makes use of blockchain technology. By contrast with traditional methods of controlling the supply of money in an economy (such as the Federal Reserve in conjunction with the United States Department of Treasury) and third parties to verify transactions (such as your local bank, credit card issuer, and the merchant's bank), Bitcoin's blockchain acts as a public ledger of all transactions throughout the history of the cryptocurrency. When a party uses that ledger, they can establish that they own the Bitcoin that they're attempting to use, and it may assist to prevent fraud and other unauthorized meddling with the money. It may also enable peer-to-peer money transfers (such as those between participants in two different countries) more efficient and less costly than conventional currency swaps, which need the involvement of a third-party organization to process the transaction.

Ethereum

Almost every major exchange will allow for the purchase of Ethereum in return for fiat cash as well as for exchange with Bitcoin. If Bitcoin ruled the cryptocurrency sector from 2008 to 2016, Ethereum has unquestionably established its presence in 2017. This comparably young cryptocurrency has made an instant impression on the sector by introducing some fantastic technical advances that have the potential to be ground-breaking and game-changing in their respective industries. It is important to note that Ethereum is not a cryptocurrency in and of itself; rather, it is a blockchain-based platform. On the other hand, tokens denominated in "ether" are exchanged on a variety of cryptocurrency exchanges. They may be used to make payments on the Ethereum blockchain and can also be traded for other cryptocurrencies or fiat money.

Many online articles may use the names "Ethereum" and "Ether" interchangeably, as will many publications in print. When it comes to groundbreaking technology known as "smart contracts," Ethereum is a standout performer. According to some, this technology has the potential to eliminate the need for attorneys and accountants. These contracts, which are made possible via the use of blockchain technology, are programmable contracts that can be configured to execute automatically whenever a certain set of circumstances is satisfied. For example, after person A completes a job for person B, an automated deposit of ten ether might be put into person A's wallet without the need for further action.

Ethereum has reached half of the market value of bitcoin, which is something that should not be taken lightly. Ethereum enjoys the second spot of cryptocurrencies by market cap, following right behind bitcoin and leaving all other cryptos way behind. Ethereum network has the power of more than six times that of bitcoin, and its smart contracts are increasingly used in partnership with well-known companies. Ethereum is quite popular among the ICO (Initial Coin Offering) crowd and many new tokens are sold on its platform. The competition between bitcoin and Ethereum seems very tight, as both cryptocurrencies enjoy a similar amount of attention.

Cardano

Cardano describes itself as a third-generation blockchain platform, in order to position itself as a next-generation participant in the space. Cardano is based on proof-of-stake, which eliminates the need for the difficult proof-of-work computations and significant power consumption needed for mining currencies like Bitcoin. This might make Cardano's network more efficient and sustainable in the long run. Cardano's cryptocurrency is named ADA after Ada Lovelace, a 19th-century mathematician who inspired the development of the cryptocurrency. Identity management and traceability are two of Cardano's most important uses. The first application may be used to expedite the acquisition of data from a variety of different sources and sources. Both of these technologies may be used to audit a product's production route and, in certain cases, to prevent fraud and counterfeit items from being produced. With the purpose of growing the network into a decentralized application (dApp) platform with a multi-asset ledger and verifiable smart contracts, Cardano is being created in five stages to achieve its goal.

Each phase, or era, of the Cardano roadmap is underpinned by a research-based methodology and peer-reviewed findings that have contributed to the development of the cryptocurrency's academic reputation. An international team of mathematicians, engineers, and cryptographers developed Cardano via a research-based approach to digital currency development. When compared to the other cryptocurrencies in the cryptocurrency ecosystem, Cardano asserts that it is a more sustainable and balanced coin.

Cardano is one of the biggest cryptocurrencies in the world with a lot of potential for growth if the circumstances are right.

Ripple XRP

One of the biggest cryptocurrencies in terms of market value is one that most investors and news organizations are unaware of. Ripple, which was founded in 2012 and operates as a payment network and protocol, aspires to make global financial transactions "safe, near instantaneous, and almost free." Transactions on the Ripple network are now completed in an average of 4 seconds.

The ultimate purpose of the platform is to render obsolete outmoded payment systems such as SWIFT and Western Union, which have long transaction times and hefty transaction costs. Ripple's payment infrastructure is already in use by a large number of global financial institutions, including heavyweights such as BBVA, Bank of America, and UBS. For example, utilizing Ripple's payment network, banks could convert currencies effortlessly, even for obscure nations and currencies such as the translation of Albanian Lek to Vietnamese Dong, which is a difficult conversion to do.

This would also eliminate the need for intermediate currencies such as the United States dollar or the Euro, among others. Banks may save an average of $3.76 each transaction by switching to the Ripple platform, according to the company. Ripple is off to a solid start, thanks to widespread acceptance in the global financial industry. This is especially true if you approach it in the same way, you would a conventional business. Ripple also has the biggest amount of coin tokens (known as XRP) accessible of any cryptocurrency, with 100 billion (of which 39 billion are available to the general public). By comparison, Bitcoin only has 16 million and Ethereum only has 94 million coins tokens available. Unlike many other cryptocurrencies, Ripple's source code is not open source. Instead, it is privately held.

Ripple Labs, Inc. is the company that produced XRP. Furthermore, although some individuals use the phrases XRP and Ripple interchangeably, the two concepts are distinct from one another. Ripple is a worldwide money transfer network that is used by financial services businesses to send money throughout the world. XRP is the cryptocurrency that was created specifically for use on the Ripple network. It is possible to purchase XRP as an investment, as a currency to be exchanged for other cryptocurrencies, or as a means of financing transactions on the Ripple blockchain.

The cryptocurrency XRP, in contrast to Bitcoin and many other cryptocurrencies, cannot be mined; instead, there is only a finite quantity of coins available — around 100 billion XRP — that have already been created. Furthermore, unlike Bitcoin and other cryptocurrencies, XRP does not depend on a complicated digital verification procedure through the blockchain, as do Bitcoin and others. Unlike other networks, the Ripple network uses an innovative approach for authenticating transactions that involves all participants conducting a poll to confirm the validity of transactions. As a result, XRP transactions are both quicker and less expensive than Bitcoin transactions. XRP, formerly known as Ripple, was established in 2012 and allows users to make payments in a variety of real-world currencies. Ripple may be beneficial in cross-border transactions since it offers a trust-less technique to make payments more convenient for both parties. XRP is a digital currency that is based on the Ripple Net digital payment infrastructure, which was developed by the business Ripple. For financial organizations looking to spread digital payments throughout the world while also lowering transaction costs associated with traditional cross-border cash transfers, this solution was created. It is also possible to extend short-term lines of credit using XRP.

Solana

Known as Solana, a blockchain platform, it is responsible for the creation of the cryptocurrency Sol. A volatile currency in recent years, the Sol increased about 60x the worth in 2021. It is one of the most volatile currencies in recent years. Its increasing prominence in the crypto sphere raises the question of why. With its decentralized finance (also known as Defib) and, more especially, its smart contract technology, which are programmers that execute on the platform in accordance with certain circumstances, Solana has achieved significant gains (like paper contracts, but without the middlemen). Additionally, Solana was behind the "Degenerate Ape Academy," which was introduced in August 2021 as a non-fungible token (NFT). Solana is a newer cryptocurrency that was launched in March 2020. It is known for its quickness in processing transactions as well as the general resilience of its "web-scale" infrastructure. SOL coins are limited to a total of 480 million coins, which is the maximum number of coins that may be issued.

The market cap of the currency is currently leaving most competitors behind, which raises the question of where it will end up.

Dogecoin

Dogecoin is a cryptocurrency that started as a joke coin based on the Doge meme. It quickly gained a large following and has nowadays a market cap exceeding most other coins. Despite its satirical tone, some people regard it as a viable investment prospect. The name comes from the popular "Doge" Internet meme, portraying a Shiba Inu dog which has been popularized by an online community called Reddit.

Even though it started out as a joke, Dogecoin has quickly gained traction among the cryptocurrency community. It was known for its tipping system which encouraged online communities to share content with one another. The community plays an important role in the coin's growth and often promotes contests for charities or other good causes.

The coin saw its value surge after obtaining endorsement from Tesla CEO Elon Musk in December 2020. Musk was successful in causing a stir in the already volatile cryptocurrency market by endorsing the meme coin. He stated in a tweet that "Dogecoin might be my fav cryptocurrency. It's pretty cool." This led to the coin's price surging by 10%.

The many reasons for its success are mainly because of its fast transaction times and easy mining. One can expect their Doge payment to arrive at the other end within just minutes, while big cryptocurrencies like Bitcoin may take an hour or more before confirmation. Mining Dogecoin is easy compared to Bitcoin because of its proof-of-work algorithm. Dogecoin, in contrast to many other digital currencies, does not have a restriction on the number of coins that may be issued, but for now the yearly growth is capped.

Litecoin

Litecoin is actually quite similar to Bitcoin, but it's cheaper and faster. Litecoin's main advantage over Bitcoin is that it processes transactions about four times faster than bitcoin does, with a block time of roughly 2.5 minutes as opposed to bitcoin's 10 minutes. There are also roughly four times as many Litecoins in circulation than there are Bitcoins.

Aside from that, Litecoin has one of the most active development teams in the whole cryptocurrency industry, enabling the coin to undergo frequent cutting-edge improvements such as becoming the first cryptocurrency to embrace Segregated Witness (SegWit) technology. This also provides the currency with the benefit of being the second most secure blockchain behind Bitcoin itself, which is a significant advantage. Another benefit for would-be investors is the rapid acceptance on major exchanges of the cryptocurrency. Litecoin purchases in fiat currency are now supported by almost all of the largest cryptocurrency exchanges, including Coinbase. This is excellent news for investors in the United States and the European Union. In terms of market behavior, Bitcoin and Litecoin usually follow a similar trend in terms of both growth and falls in the value of their respective currencies. For the purpose of diversifying their portfolio, many investors pick Litecoin as a supplemental choice to Bitcoin.

For those who are interested in mining, Litecoin's algorithm is significantly simpler than Bitcoin's process, which lowers the mining expenses and entrance hurdles. The Script algorithm is used by Litecoin, while the SHA-256 method is used by Bitcoin. The biggest practical implication of this is that Script requires less processing power from graphics processing units, resulting in cheaper mining costs (GPUs). For the amateur or home-based miner in 2017, Bitcoin mining is no longer a realistic choice. However, even when power costs are taken into consideration in first world nations, the Litecoin mining industry may still generate a profit. Detractors of Litecoin have accused the cryptocurrency of being "simply another Bitcoin with no innovation." In addition, the currency was the victim of a Chinese pump and dump fraud in 2015, in which speculators amassed 22 percent of all the coins in circulation before selling them.

Polygon / Matic

Polygon, formerly known as Matic Network, is a framework for creating linked blockchain networks that is open source. It aims to overcome some of Ethereum's key shortcomings, such as its throughput, bad user experience (high speed and delayed transactions), and lack of community control, by implementing a revolutionary sidechain solution on top of the Ethereum blockchain.

Polygon, as opposed to its predecessor Matic Network, which used a technology known as Plasma to process transactions off-chain before finalizing them on the Ethereum main chain, is intended to be an entire platform for the development of interoperable blockchains, rather than a simple scaling solution. Developers may use Polygon to establish pre-configured blockchain networks with features that are suited to their specific requirements. Additionally, an increasing number of modules are available, allowing developers to build sovereign blockchains that provide more particular functionality. Polygon's design may be best described as a four-tier system, with the Ethereum layer at the top, the security layer below it, the Polygon networks layer below it, and the execution layer below it. The Ethereum layer is, in essence, a collection of smart contracts that are deployed on the Ethereum platform. In addition to handling transaction finality, staking and communication between Ethereum and the multiple Polygon chains, smart contracts also perform other tasks. Ethereum's security layer operates in the background alongside Ethereum and performs the function of "validators as a service," which enables chains to benefit from an extra layer of protection. Both the Ethereum and the Security layers are entirely up to the user.

There are two further levels that must be completed. The first of these layers is the Polygon networks layer, which is the ecosystem of blockchain networks that are constructed on top of the Polygon technology. Each of them has its own community, which is in charge of achieving local agreement and constructing blocks of various sizes. Polygon's Ethereum Virtual Machine (EVM) implementation is utilized for smart contract execution at the second tier, which is known as the Execution layer in this case. Because of Polygon's arbitrary message passing features, chains created on Polygon are capable of talking with one another as well as with the Ethereum main chain, allowing them to collaborate on projects. Various new use-cases, such as interoperable decentralized applications (dApps) and the easy exchange of money across varied platforms, will be made possible as a result of this development. A future in which separate blockchains no longer function as closed-off silos and private communities, but rather as networks that are integrated into a greater linked environment, is the goal of Polygon. Its long-term objective is to create an open, borderless world in which consumers can effortlessly connect with decentralized goods and services without first having to pass via intermediaries or walled gardens, which is currently the only way to do this. It hopes to provide a central hub into which other blockchains may easily plug in, while also addressing some of their specific shortcomings—such as excessive fees, poor scalability, and insufficient security—at the same time.

Binance Coin

In addition to being one of the largest cryptocurrency exchanges in the world, Binary Coin (BNB) is a cryptocurrency token that was designed to be used as a medium of exchange on the cryptocurrency exchange Binance. However, it is currently hosted on Binance's own blockchain platform, which was originally constructed on the Ethereum blockchain. BNB was first launched as a utility token in 2017 to enable traders to get savings on trading costs on Binance; however, it is also capable of being used for a variety of other purposes, including payments, trip booking, entertainment, online services, and even financial services.

BNB was launched with a maximum of 200 million tokens, of which about half were made accessible to investors during its initial coin offering (ICO). Every quarter, Binance buys back and then "burns," or permanently destroys, part of the tokens it has in order to keep demand high and so increase its value. Binance conducted its 16th burn in July 2021, burning around 1.29 million BNB, which was roughly equivalent to $394 million at the time. At the time of writing, this is the third biggest cryptocurrency by market capitalization.

Shiba Inu coin

Shiba Inu Coin is a decentralized cryptocurrency that promotes community development and is being created as "an experiment" inside the Shiba Inu Ecosystem. They constructed it on top of the Ethereum Blockchain Network, which is also used by many other digital currencies. It is a meme currency that was created as a competitor to Dogecoin, often known as "Doge-Killer." It has already taken over several Dogecoin marketplaces and is quickly becoming a popular option among investors in the cryptocurrency industry.

Shiba Inu, established in August 2020, is a joke coin or meme coin that was released as a direct competitor to Dogecoin in the cryptocurrency market. The Shiba Inu has been in the headlines for a couple of different reasons. Recently, Tesla creator Elon Musk tweeted that he would want to purchase a Shiba dog, which sparked interest in the cryptocurrency market, resulting in a 300 percent increase in the price of some altcoins. Shiba Inu is originally the Japanese dog breed that inspired the creation of several meme coins. Designed after the Shiba dog, the Shiba Inu mascot is very similar to the Dogecoin mascot in both appearance and personality. At the moment, there is no real application for the Shina Inu coin other than being funny. That might change of course in the future.

Tether

Tether was the first cryptocurrency to be promoted as a stablecoin, which is a kind of cryptocurrency that is tied to a fiat-currency. Tether, like other stablecoins, is intended to provide users with more stability, transparency, and reduced transaction fees than other cryptocurrencies. Instead of being a high-risk speculative investment like certain cryptocurrencies, Tether may be utilized by investors who wish to escape the tremendous volatility that characterizes the cryptocurrency industry. Tethers were used in 57 percent of bitcoin transactions in the beginning of 2021. Tether is pegged to the United States dollar (thus the symbol USDT), and it is believed to retain a 1:1 value with the dollar, but this claim has come under considerable suspicion. There is no assurance offered by Tether, Ltd. for any redemption of Tethers, which means that it could happen that they cannot be exchanged for dollars. The market cap on the other hand is rapidly increasing. Be aware of the risks with this currency.

Monero

It is possible to send and receive payments with Monero without having to worry about a public transaction record being made accessible on the blockchain. By default, all Monero transactions are kept confidential. If you place a high value on privacy first and foremost, Monero will meet all of your requirements. The money has been intended to be completely anonymous and untraceable at all times.

This extends to their development staff, which, in contrast to other cryptocurrencies, does not have a public CEO or leader. Monero also makes use of "ring signatures," a sort of encryption that is unique to the cryptocurrency, to guarantee that transactions are untraceable. Users will be able to receive money without being able to connect the address to the sender in this manner. Because of the nature of anonymity, this might be seen both beneficial and detrimental depending on your point of view. In addition to concealing the identities of the buyer and seller, the ring signatures also disguise the value of the transaction.

In contrast to Dash, Monero has been open source from its birth, allowing anybody to inspect the source code and ensure complete transparency. Because of the currency's anonymity, it has become a favorite among those who use the dark web. Before it was shut down, the darknet market site AlphaBay used both Monero and Bitcoin to handle transactional fees on its transactions. The network was used to sell anything from illicit narcotics to weapons to stolen credit cards, among other things. Monero's anonymity has also made it a popular among ransomware hackers, who use it to hide their identities. It remains to be seen if Monero will be expanded to include more legitimate applications, such as the ability to disguise one's genuine net worth. Alternatively, whether it will continue to be the preferred coin of more illicit industries, preventing it from achieving widespread adoption in comparison to other coins. This uncertainty could be used to the advantage of speculators who are looking to profit from the potential for widespread adoption.

Polkadot

In the blockchain world, Polkadot is a next-generation protocol that connects numerous specialized blockchains into a single, unified network. Polkadot is a blockchain network that was created as part of a larger vision for the web that gives people back control over internet monopolies. It builds on the revolutionary promise of prior blockchain networks while also providing numerous essential benefits. The amount of bandwidth that can be processed by blockchains in isolation is restricted. Polkadot is a sharded multichain network, which means that it can process many transactions on several chains in parallel, eliminating the bottlenecks that occurred on legacy networks that processed transactions one at a time. This is in contrast to legacy networks that processed transactions one by one. This increase in parallel processing capacity has a substantial impact on scalability, and it has the potential to generate favorable circumstances for further adoption and future growth. Due to the fact that they execute on the network in parallel, sharded chains linked to Polkadot are referred to as "Para chains."

When it comes to blockchain architecture, there is no such thing as one size fits all. Every blockchain makes sacrifices in order to accommodate a variety of features and use cases. In the case of identity management, one chain may be optimized for this, while another may be optimized for file storage. A new design for each blockchain on Polkadot may be tailored for a particular use case, allowing each blockchain to be unique. In other words, blockchains can provide better services while simultaneously enhancing efficiency and security by eliminating redundant code from the system. By using the Substrate development platform, teams can design and configure their blockchains more quickly and effectively than they have ever been able to do previously. Using Polkadot, networks and applications may exchange information and functionality in the same way as apps on a smartphone do, without the need to depend on centralized service providers with dubious data privacy policies. Polkadot, in contrast to prior networks that mostly functioned as stand-alone settings, allows for interoperability and communication across several chains. This opens the door to new and creative services, as well as the ability for users to transmit information across networks. For example, a chain offering financial services may interact with another chain that gives access to real-world data (known as an oracle chain), such as stock market price feeds for tokenized equities trading or a network that offers access to real-world data for cryptocurrency mining.

USD Coin

USD Coin, usually known by its cryptocurrency ticker symbol USDC, is a stablecoin that has a fixed value of one dollar per coin, and each USD Coin is backed by one dollar in a separate bank account. As a result, USD Coin has become a popular alternative among cryptocurrency investors who wish to avoid the volatility and price risk associated with major currencies such as Bitcoin and Ethereum.

A cooperation between Circle and Coinbase resulted in the launching of this cryptocurrency on September 2018. USDC is a cryptocurrency that competes with Tether (USDT) and Trues (TUSD). The USD Coin service, in its most basic form, is a service that tokenizes US dollars and makes them available for usage on the internet and public blockchains. Furthermore, USDC tokens may be exchanged for US dollars at any point in time. The USDC coins are issued and redeemed in accordance with the terms of the ERC-20 smart contract.

Terra (Luna)

Terra (LUNA) is a blockchain protocol for issuing algorithmic stablecoins and building decentralized financial infrastructure. You may earn interest on stablecoins, spend cryptocurrency with merchants, and replace the majority of your banking requirements using Terra as a single DeFi protocol. To fulfill its basic purpose as a stablecoin platform, Terra employs an elegant mechanism to keep a tight fiat currency peg.

Terra, on the other hand, does much more than just create stablecoins. It's also a smart contract-enabled blockchain with a developing DeFi ecosystem linked to the Cosmos IBC protocol. Terra's goal is to replace banks, credit networks, and payment systems like PayPal with one uninterrupted and gratifying blockchain experience over time.

With the issuance of stablecoins on the platform, the project has gained widespread attention in a short period of time. TerraUSD has already surpassed many stablecoins in terms of market capitalization as of this writing. When it comes to collateralizing fiat-backed stablecoins and crypto-backed stablecoins, stablecoins on the Terra network employ a somewhat different mechanism. Typically, holders of collateralized stablecoins are able to trade their stablecoins for a comparable quantity of fiat currency or a certain amount of cryptocurrency. Each stablecoins is, in effect, backed by and exchangeable for the LUNA utility token, which serves as both a governance and utility token. When someone wants to exchange their stablecoins for LUNA or vice versa, Terra serves as a counterparty for them, and this has an impact on the supply of both tokens.

Avalanche

Avalanche is a layer one blockchain that serves as a foundation for decentralized apps and bespoke blockchain networks. It is still under development. It is a competitor to Ethereum, and it is attempting to dethrone Ethereum as the most popular blockchain for smart contracts. To do this, it intends to have a larger transaction output of up to 6,500 transactions per second while maintaining excellent scalability. This is made feasible by the one-of-a-kind architecture of Avalanche. This network is made up of three independent blockchains: the X-Chain, the C-Chain, and the P-Chain, all of which are linked together by the P-Chain.

Each chain serves a specific function, which is a significant departure from the strategy used by Bitcoin and Ethereum, which is to have all nodes verify all transactions simultaneously. Avalanche blockchains even use a variety of different consensus processes, depending on their intended function. Following the introduction of its mainnet in 2020, Avalanche has been hard at work establishing its own ecosystem of DApps and DeFi. Avalanche has been connected with a number of other Ethereum-based applications, including SushiSwap and TrueUSD. As an added bonus, the platform is continually attempting to improve interoperability between its own ecosystem and Ethereum by, for example, developing bridges between the two networks.

Chainlink

A currency based on the Ethereum blockchain, Chainlink (LINK) is used to fuel the Chainlink decentralized oracle network. Connecting to external data sources, application programming interfaces, and payment systems via this network is possible for smart contracts on Ethereum. A blockchain oracle network based on the Ethereum blockchain, Chainlink is a decentralized database of information. The network is designed to be used to enable the movement of tamper-proof data from off-chain sources to smart contracts running on the Ethereum blockchain itself. In the words of its creators, it can be used to verify whether the parameters of a smart contract are met in a way that is completely independent of any of the contract's stakeholders. This is accomplished by "connecting the contract directly to real-world data, events, payments, and other inputs," according to the developers."

Store Crypto in Wallets

You'll need a secure place to keep your cryptocurrency once you've successfully purchased it, whether it's Bitcoin, Ethereum, or another altcoin. When it comes to spending money, your cryptocurrency wallet is similar to a traditional fiat currency wallet in that you may use it to track precisely how much money you have on hand. But because of the technology that underpins how cryptocurrency coins are minted, cryptocurrency wallets are distinct from fiat money wallets. Because of the way bitcoin works, it is not held in a single area. Within the blockchain, this information is kept safe and secure for future reference. A public record of ownership for each coin exists, and when a transaction happens, the ownership record is updated to reflect the new ownership information.

When dealing with cryptocurrencies, people utilize a crypto wallet as a secure depository as well as a payment instrument for both incoming and outgoing payments, respectively. Let's take a look at the many types of wallets that are available and choose which one is the most appropriate for your needs. When it comes to storing money, cold wallets (offline) are employed. Hot wallets (online) are used for sending and receiving cash swiftly.

A wallet typically has two keys: a private key and a public key. The Private key should be only available to you and you should never share it with anyone else while you are holding your assets. It is essential that you keep this in mind while signing transactions with your keys. It is completely safe on the other hand to share your public keys with someone else, to transfer crypto to your account, for example. This key may even be made public via social media platforms for whatever reason.

To share your public key with anybody is completely secure. Users with access to your public key are only able to make deposits into your account. You may transmit bitcoin to others via the use of your private key on the other hand. The public key of the receiver and the private key of the sender are both utilized in every transaction. In the event of a hard-ware failure or data theft, it is recommended that you keep an offline backup of your private key. Anyone who has access to your private key will be able to remove money from your account, which brings us to the first rule of bitcoin and crypto storage: keep your private key safe at all costs.

Hot Storage Wallet

A hot wallet is a type of wallet that is connected to the Internet. It usually contains a small number of coins for daily transactions and spending, and its primary purpose is to hold the funds that you need fairly quickly. This is an important distinction from a hardware wallet or cold storage solution, which hold your private keys in a secure offline environment.

Much like a checking account in your real life, a hot wallet should not contain too much money at any given time because it could be lost very easily if somehow compromised. Best practices dictate that you should only keep as much money in your hot wallet as you expect to use for day-to-day transactions. You may also want to consider segregating the funds in your main wallet into 2-3 hot wallets, with each one containing an increasingly larger amount (if you need more than 3 wallets, try using sub-wallets).

You should also backup your keys regularly to avoid losing access to your funds. If you lose one of the 2-3 wallets, it will not be too much of an inconvenience but if you lose them all, it might be hard getting back access to your coins.

A hot wallet is very convenient for quick transactions and daily use, but you should always keep in mind that it may be comprised by malware or hackers. Because of this possibility, if you store a large number of coins in any one hot wallet, we highly recommend validating all outgoing transactions with a second device (such as a computer).

Use different passwords (3+) for each hot wallet (and especially for each exchange). If you use the same password on all of your wallets/exchanges, then you risk losing all of your funds if one is compromised.

For bigger accounts only use exchanges that are transparent and have a long history of successful operations and customer satisfaction. Only use exchanges that provide proof-of-reserve audits to ensure your funds are 100% backed by actual assets in the exchange's reserve.

Most importantly, don't store large amounts of money on a hot wallet. If you want to use a hot wallet as your main wallet, then it should only contain an amount that you're fine with losing if your device gets destroyed or stolen.

You typically see hot wallets as mobile apps or desktop software that you download, but an online wallet would be the equivalent of your bank's web app.

Cold Storage Wallet

If you want to be on the safe side (hacking is a big issue), the apparent solution is cold storage or offline wallets, which are available in two broad variants: paper and hardware wallets. Before I go into detail about how these two types of cold storages function, allow me to explain how cryptocurrency storage, specifically blockchain storage, works. In order to facilitate the purchase of cryptocurrency on any given exchange, your transaction is allocated a public key that is associated with the number unit(s) of cryptocurrency that you purchased.

While your cryptocurrency exchange assigns private keys that match to your public keys, your cryptocurrency wallet does not. So, your private keys are the lifeline that keeps your cryptocurrencies alive. If you misplace or forget them, you may as well say goodbye to your cryptocurrencies altogether. In order for someone to effectively "take" your cryptocurrency, they must first have access to your public and private keys. It's similar to your ATM card's personal identification number in that it will enable other individuals to take money from your account without your knowledge or consent. When you keep your cryptocurrencies in your hot wallet, which is your cryptocurrency exchange account, you put yourself and your funds at danger of being hacked and your funds stolen. In order to prevent this from happening, as soon as you have finished purchasing your crypto, you should move it, together with your private keys, to your cold storage or offline wallet. I'll discuss how the paper wallets and hardware wallets function now that we've covered the basics of their operation. The paper wallet isn't truly a wallet, but rather a backup for your wallet. Write down your private keys on a piece of paper and keep that piece of paper in a location where it is practically impossible to steal or destroy the keys. A fireproof safe is an excellent location to store valuables. Another kind of safe is a safety deposit box. Hardware wallets are USB-type devices that you may use to store your coins as well as their respective private keys.

These are devices which main function is to store your cryptocurrency, and as a result, they are often unplugged for the vast majority of the time. In order to use them to receive or transfer your bitcoins from and to your cryptocurrency exchange account for the purpose of conducting transactions, all you have to do is plug them into the USB port of your Internet-connected desktop or laptop computer and follow the on-screen instructions. Cold storage hardware wallets are far safer than software wallets, which are programs loaded on mobile devices, for a variety of reasons. A major concern is that if it's put on a gadget that is mostly used online, the likelihood of it being hacked remains high. Second of all, even if you install it on a device that will only be used for cryptocurrency transactions, there is still a risk of loss if that computer is damaged beyond repair or, even if it can still be repaired, the computer technician to whom you will be entrusting the repair may be able to hack the drive and, as a result, your wallet. When using a hardware cold storage wallet, the chance of losing your private keys as a result of hardware failure is significantly reduced. Furthermore, utilizing a paper wallet as a backup may assist to reduce the likelihood of such a danger.

Paper wallets are nothing more than a collection of notes containing your private key that are written down on paper. They will often include QR codes, allowing the sender to rapidly scan them and deliver bitcoin to the recipient. Due to the fact that your private keys are not saved in a digital format, they cannot be compromised by cyber-attacks or device failure. It is advised that you store your paper wallet in a sealed plastic bag to keep it safe from moisture or other adverse circumstances. If you want to keep your bitcoin for a lengthy period of time, keep the paper in a secure place. Before printing any paper wallets, make sure you have thoroughly read and comprehended the step-by-step instructions. The term "hardware wallet" refers to physical storage devices that have your private key in their memory. The most prevalent kind of these are encrypted USB sticks, which are available on the market. Two-factor authentication, often known as 2FA, is used by these wallets to guarantee that only the wallet owner has access to the data.

If you have a physical USB stick inserted into your computer, one element is the actual USB stick, and the other is a four-digit pin number, the process is quite similar to how you take money from an ATM using a debit card.

Trusting that the supplier would offer a wallet that has not been used. The use of a second-hand wallet constitutes a significant security violation. Hardware wallets should only be purchased from authorized vendors Alternative cryptocurrencies that are not supported by these wallets may be stored in an encrypted USB wallet that can be created by following a coin specific guide.

Private/ Public Keys

Asymmetric cryptography, sometimes known as public-key cryptography, is a kind of cryptographic system that makes use of pairs of keys. Identical public and private keys are used to create each pair. Such key pairs are generated via cryptographic algorithms that are based on mathematical problems known as one-way functions, which are described in more detail below. As previously stated, public and private keys serve as the foundation for public key cryptography, which is also known as asymmetric cryptography. In public key cryptography, each public key corresponds to a single private key, and vice versa. They are used in conjunction to encrypt and decode communications.

In the case of encrypting a communication using a person's public key, they can only decrypt it using their corresponding public and private keys. The public key has been compared to a company's web address in that it is available for anybody to see, as well as for them to distribute widely. The public keys used in asymmetric encryption are available for use by anybody else in the system. Once the sender has obtained the public key, he may use it to encrypt the message being sent. Each public key is accompanied by a corresponding private key that is distinct from the others. Consider a private key to be similar to the key to the front door of a company, except that only you have a copy of the key. One of the most significant distinctions between the two sorts of keys is defined by this. The private key guarantees that only you and your guests may get entry via the front door. In the event of encrypted communications, you will need to utilize this private key in order to decode them. These keys work together to help guarantee the security of the information that is transferred. A communication that has been encrypted with the public key cannot be decoded unless the matching private key is also used.

Keep Crypto safe

The majority of the threats to your digital money come from cryptocurrency wallets (also known as digital wallets) and exchange providers. It is not your digital coins that are stored in a crypto wallet; rather, it is your private key, which enables you to exchange cryptocurrencies online. This private key serves as your digital identity in the cryptocurrency market, and anybody who has access to it has the ability to carry out fraudulent transactions or steal your bitcoin money. When cybercriminals hack digital wallets, they use sophisticated tactics to steal or move cryptocurrency assets without the user's awareness.

When it comes to safeguarding your digital money from cyberattacks, the security of your wallet is critical to success. Cold wallets, in contrast to hot wallets, do not have a connection to the internet, making them less vulnerable to hackers. Storing your private keys in a cold wallet, also known as a hardware wallet, is the most secure choice since these wallets are encrypted, which ensures that your keys are kept safe at all times. In January 2019, the Japanese cryptocurrency exchange Bipoint detected an unlawful withdrawal of $32 million from its hot wallet in several cryptocurrencies, which had been targeting more than 50,000 customers at the time. Bitcoin, Bitcoin Cash, Ethereum, Litecoin, and Ripple were among the cryptocurrencies handled by the exchange in its hot wallet. Bipoint, on the other hand, has stated that the issue did not have an impact on their cold wallet or cash balances. When trading or doing cryptocurrency transactions, always utilize a secure internet connection and avoid connecting to public Wi-Fi networks, if at all possible. Even while connecting to your home network, a virtual private network (VPN) may provide extra protection.

A virtual private network (VPN) masks your IP address and geographic location, keeping your surfing activities secure and hidden from malicious actors. It's impossible to overstate the significance of a strong password when it comes to information security. Three-quarters of millennials in the United States, according to a recent research, use the same password on more than ten different devices, applications, and other social media accounts.

According to the report, the vast majority of them were using the same password in more than 50 different sites. Always choose a strong and complicated password that is difficult to guess, and change it on a regular basis to keep your information safe. If you have many wallets, use different passwords for each one. Choose two-factor authentication (2FA) or multi-factor authentication (MFA) to increase the level of protection available. Phishing schemes, which are spread via harmful advertisements and emails, are common in the bitcoin sector. When doing cryptocurrency transactions, use caution and avoid clicking on any strange or unfamiliar URLs. In a recent cryptocurrency heist, the hacker gang "Crypto Core" used spear-phishing tactics to target cryptocurrency exchanges and steal bitcoin. During the course of two years, attackers have stolen bitcoin worth $200 million from firms in the United States and Japan, according to reports. The cryptocurrency exchange's staff and security executives were identified during a reconnaissance phase, according to Clear Sky, before a spear-phishing assault was launched against them. These assaults were carried out via the use of bogus websites that impersonated linked businesses and workers, as well as the insertion of harmful URLs in documents through the use of emails. In this ever-evolving business of cryptocurrencies, it is your alone obligation to safeguard your digital cash by safeguarding your wallet with the most basic of security procedures. Make sure you're up to speed on the newest security developments, including attack methodologies and preventive measures.

Handle Crypto

For many investors, cryptocurrencies have been nothing short of a thrilling experience. They have a natural appeal: they have risen significantly in value, and investors are attracted to them by the seemingly substantial profits on offer. Because of their volatility, they also provide several chances for individuals who like to speculate on price swings. If you want to give it a go, these are the steps you should follow. You have the option of either purchasing bitcoin units or trading on the price of cryptocurrencies. Through the use of cryptocurrency ETFs and CFDs, you may speculate on the price of a cryptocurrency without ever having to purchase any of the underlying assets. When you purchase a cryptocurrency unit, you are obligated to pay the whole purchase price of the asset. When trading, you only have to put up a tiny part of the entire amount of money you want to invest. The ability to leverage your position on the price enables you to get a higher exposure than would otherwise be possible with your initial investment amount.

This method may also be less expensive since investors do not have to pay any deposit or withdrawal fees in order to access the currency, for example. Trading has a variety of tax benefits over investing, and this is one of them. If you benefit by trading cryptocurrencies, you will not be subject to capital gains taxes, however if you earn from purchasing and selling cryptocurrencies directly, you would be. On the other side, if you make a mistake with your trading technique, the trading method might amplify your losses.

How to buy

To purchase cryptocurrency, you must create an account at an exchange, where you may also sell it. For beginners, you have to start with one that accepts fiat money. Before trading, you must ensure that you are familiar with and understand your market. A very diverse range of variables influences the price of cryptocurrency. Price movements have been impacted in the last year by fears about government regulation, media coverage of the industry, and the fortunes of the US dollar - in addition to pronouncements from significant corporate executives or government officials. The greater the number of individuals who get interested with cryptocurrencies, the greater the influence of these many elements will grow. To purchase cryptocurrency, you must first ensure that you have sufficient cash in your account. You may fund your cryptocurrency account by connecting it to your bank account, allowing a wire transfer, or even making a payment using a debit or credit card, among other methods.

Depending on the exchange or broker you choose, as well as your financing method, you may have to wait a few days before you can utilize the funds you deposit to purchase cryptocurrencies on their exchange. Here's one major buyer beware point: It is possible to deposit money with a credit card at certain exchanges or brokers, but this is exceedingly risky—and also quite costly. Credit card issuers see bitcoin transactions made using credit cards as cash advances, according to the Federal Reserve. They will thus be subject to higher interest rates than conventional purchases, and you will also be required to pay extra cash advance costs on top of that. When you get a cash advance, for example, you may be required to pay a fee of 5 percent of the whole transaction amount. This is on top of any costs that your cryptocurrency exchange or brokerage may impose, which may total up to 5 percent of your cryptocurrency buy, meaning you might lose up to 10% of your cryptocurrency purchase to fees.

How to sell

It is expected that you will be able to trade all of the main currencies like Bitcoin and Ethereum on the major platforms and that new currencies will be introduced all of the time. There's a good chance you won't be able to trade all the numerous different cryptocurrencies, at least if you went for the exotic ones. Choosing cryptos that are actually being traded might be preferable over buying all available meme coins because they are funny.

How to send and receive crypto

You may utilize your wallets or online accounts to transmit and receive supported cryptocurrencies if your wallets are compatible. Sending and receiving messages is possible on both mobile and online devices.

To transfer or receive cryptocurrency, you must first get a cryptocurrency wallet, after which you must enter the public address of the person to whom you want to send or receive bitcoin (or give your public address and have someone else put it in to receive). The process may sometimes be simplified by scanning the QR code associated with the receiving location and entering the amount you want to transfer; however, if you do not have a QR code, copying and pasting the public address is the next best option. It's as simple as selecting the amount you wish to transfer, following any additional wallet-specific instructions (for example, adding money for fees if required), and then pressing send (or the equivalent button on your wallet) to complete the transaction. As soon as it is completed, the transaction just has to be confirmed on the blockchain (how long that takes can differ between blockchains and depend on how much you paid in fees). If you are concerned about the status of the transaction on the blockchain, you can always use the block explorer for the currency that you transferred to see how it is progressing.

Crypto Investing and Trading

When it comes to buying crypto, you can either approach it as an investor or a trader. The two are not mutually exclusive, but there is a big difference. An investor is someone who buys cryptocurrencies with the intention of holding for months or years, while traders generally hold smaller positions (hours to days) and use leverage wherever they can to make gains on their investment. If you are starting out, I would strongly recommend you go the investor route to learn as much as possible before trading. Each investor has their own strategy, but the important thing is to stay informed and adapt your strategy as time goes by. Don't be afraid to change your mind. Just remember that having a plan is better than not having one!

When it comes to investing, people typically use fundamental research as a way to evaluate the value of an asset or token. However, this method does not work for cryptocurrencies since most do not have any cash flow and cannot be valued based on earnings so we need another method. Enter: Technical Analysis.

The good thing about technical analysis is that it can be applied to any market and doesn't require fundamental research. Cryptocurrencies cannot be valued based on earnings because none of them generate cash flow and thus we need a different measuring stick. Technical Analysis works by analyzing the price movements in a market and use patterns to predict future price movements.

In a later chapter we will discuss the basics of Technical Analysis and how it applies to cryptocurrencies.

How to invest in cryptocurrency

Investing should always start with a plan to stay organized and focus on what is important. In the book you will learn how to develop your own cryptocurrency investing plan so that you can invest in cryptocurrencies more successfully. Other than trading cryptocurrencies, investing in cryptocurrencies requires some deeper research. In the book I will cover all the important topics you should be aware to make an informed decision when choosing your next investment.

The cryptocurrency landscape is constantly changing and there are a lot of new things that can affect each one of them. From regulations to forks, understanding what's going on in this industry is crucial. You need to keep yourself informed so that you can make the right decision when buying or selling these digital assets.

A proper investment plan should include where your money will be invested, how much of it, and at what frequency. But before all this, you should know which cryptocurrencies are worth investing in. Some chapters in this book cover how the different currencies actually work and basics on how to do Technical Analysis. If you are planning to be an investor, you shouldn't skip over them. With the help of some simple models, you will be able to determine which cryptocurrencies are worth your hard-earned money. Once you pick a cryptocurrency in which you want to invest, you need to decide when is the best time for buying or selling it. Every investment has its own lifecycle and trying to guess when it is experiencing more growth or facing some tough times can be challenging. But fear not, by the end of this book you will know everything you need to know about investing in cryptocurrencies. You will learn how to develop your own cryptocurrency investment plan and make more informed decisions on when the best time for buying or selling has arrived.

One of the main advantages that cryptocurrencies have over other asset classes is how accessible they are. Since most people buy cryptocurrencies through exchanges, you don't need to be rich to get started... But there are some risks associated with using these services since they can close your account anytime without notice. In order to have a successful journey into the cryptocurrency landscape, you need to learn how to properly store your assets so they are not lost or stolen.

Cryptocurrency investment strategy

One of the most popular ways to invest in cryptocurrencies is holding them for a long period of time, which is described as buy and hold (Or HODL in the crypto world). By just purchasing coins and keeping them stored safely in your wallet, you can enjoy price appreciation over time without doing anything else. While this is one of the simplest investment strategies, you need to understand the risk associated with it. These assets are extremely volatile and some unexpected events can cause big price movements where you can actually lose your investment. If the cryptocurrency you hold gets hacked or there is a service outage on an exchange, your funds might get stolen or lost forever. There are also people who buy cryptocurrencies directly from miners but this usually requires some technical background and it is more expensive than the alternatives.

A better way is to aim for a long-term investment, but keep yourself up to date and react to important events that might affect your assets. The best way to do this is by creating a cryptocurrency investment plan where you list the coins you want to invest in and how much. You should also consider when to buy or sell a coin based on its performance over time. Do not get nervous on short term fluctuations, try to ignore the noise and focus on coins that have a clear potential. But if your coin turns out to be a scam, a buy and hold strategy will lose all of your money.

A cryptocurrency investment plan can be developed in several ways but it is important to highlight the goals of the person behind it. Looking for long term investments, you will need to evaluate if the coin does solve a specific problem or offer any unique service. You should also check its market capitalization and popularity to see how big of an impact it will have over time. Once you find a suitable candidate, try doing technical analysis to determine where its price might be in the future.

Another not well known but simple way to invest in cryptocurrencies is through an index fund. By spreading your investment throughout several cryptocurrencies and using their market cap as a weighting method, you don't need to worry about choosing the next coin and if it will succeed. The only question you need to answer before buying index funds are: How much can I invest? After that, just sit back and relax as your investment grows without any effort from your side.

Generally, before you make your first investment, you need to think about how much money you are willing to invest. You shouldn't borrow money in order to buy cryptocurrencies since the market is still in its infancy and it needs time for price appreciation in order for you to make any profit. Just like when picking traditional stocks during an IPO, cryptocurrency investing is no different and you need to be patient.

Do not forget that both investing in cryptocurrency assets or index funds are high risk strategies. Even if the market keeps growing, there is always a chance for everything to collapse overnight. You should never invest more than you are willing to lose so you can have an emergency fund ready in case anything bad happens.

It is highly recommended to read all the resources you can get your hands on about cryptocurrencies, their technology and how they work. You should also check if the coin you want to invest in belongs to a popular blockchain platform so it will be widely supported by developers over time. If you are looking for long term investments, create a plan and do a technical analysis to determine where a coin is going. Avoid FOMO (Fear of missing out) and market manipulation since they will just damage your investment.

How to trade cryptocurrency

Because the word "trading" is in the title, you may think that not everyone is suited for this field of work. To a certain extent, you are correct. Trading requires a good strategy and the will to stick to it. You will be successful if you are familiar with trading 101, are interested in news and events in the crypto world, and keep track of the current value of the currency. You could also learn how to generate some basic financial projections. In reality, trading on the cryptocurrency market is not that far from trading on the stock exchange in terms of complexity. Knowing how to examine charts and make well-considered judgments, as well as not succumbing to fear, rumors, or emotions, is essential. Most important of all, one must be prepared to lose money on some trades.

To be a good trader, you must possess both the intellectual and technical abilities necessary. Market charts on the performance of the listed assets will be necessary for you to make correct forecasts about price rises and declines, which will need you to evaluate market charts on the performance of the listed assets. A long or short position may be taken while trading, based on whether you believe the price of an asset will increase or decrease in the future. This implies that you may generate money regardless of whether the cryptocurrency market is bullish or bearish at any one time.

Most exchanges charge a fee every transaction, so it might be preferable to swap big quantities at once. Despite the fact that it may be frightening, it is a time-tested reality. Do not go for great risk to maximize your potential earnings, but try to preserve your capital by taking calculated risks. While it is possible for you to gain money in the short term, you must also be prepared to lose your trade within that time period. This is particularly true in a volatile market such as the cryptocurrency market. If this is happening, you need to make sure to act emotionless and close the trade before you lose the full amount. Hoping that the trade will turn into something profitable is not a very good strategy.

A perpetual balancing act and trade-off between risk and reward is required for each kind of trading decision. It is possible to categorize short-term trading into multiple categories within itself, depending on how soon you earn gains – whether it takes minutes, hours or days. Generally speaking, the shorter the time window for a trading transaction, the greater the risk associated with that transaction. Before you begin trading, you must determine if cryptocurrency trading is appropriate for your circumstances and that you are aware of the hazards connected with cryptocurrency trading.

Many beginners like to trade cryptocurrencies like a video game since it is a very volatile asset with high returns. Trading cryptocurrency may provide much larger returns than conventional investments if you are able to predict the market correctly. But if you want to survive in this market for a longer time, you need to create your own strategy. A crypto bull market makes it relatively simple for the value of your portfolio to expand, but the volatility can be brutal in both directions. Also keep in mind, that crypto can be traded 24/7, so do not leave your trades open overnight.

Cryptocurrency trading strategy

Before you begin trading, you must determine if cryptocurrency trading is appropriate for your circumstances and that you are aware of the hazards connected with cryptocurrency trading. Following these five steps first:

- Make your own study and determine whether or not the crypto space is a good fit for you (Stocks are also very interesting for trading)
- Make a decision on whether you really want to engage in short-term trading or if long-term would be a better fit for you.
- Select the trading technique / trading strategy that is most appropriate for you.
- Learn how to place trades on your platform and interpret charts to make money in the crypto market.
- Make a risk management strategy and stick to it.

The distinction between gambling and trading is the presence of a strategy. The process of developing a plan consists of three elements:

Look for patterns

The fundamental idea of reading charts and developing trading strategies is to search for patterns in recent price movements, and then use those patterns to attempt to anticipate future price changes in the market. Patterns like as resistance and support, for example, are seen often enough across numerous markets that they have been given their own names. Others, on the other hand, are far less well-known and are never given names of their own. It is possible to trade on patterns such as the belief that Bitcoin increases when Ethereum falls or that Bitcoin rises when the US dollar declines compared to the Chinese renminbi, or any other pattern you can think of.

Experiment

It's a good idea to put trading ideas through their paces before investing actual money in them. Paper trading and back testing may both be beneficial in this situation. Both of these characteristics are often observed on trading platforms. Paper trading is a method of testing a trading technique on the actual markets while using fictitious money. It allows you to test your approach in real-time, current market circumstances. In trading, back testing is the process of running a trading strategy against previous market movements to determine how it would have fared. In order to get your head around the basics of reading charts and identifying patterns, you may want to read the step-by-step guide to cryptocurrency technical analysis to get a sense of how to get started spotting patterns on the cryptocurrency market.

Define boundaries and stick to them

Cutting your losses is important, but knowing when to sell is also essential. Many people get it wrong and end up buying high and selling low.

Knowing your exit strategy will help you set boundaries, know when to sell and be disciplined about it. You should have a number in mind that if reached means the trade is no longer profitable. Exit the trade immediately!

Markets can be irrational and unpredictable, which makes it important to have a plan. Selling low and buying high is the worst mistake that future investors make.

How to profit from crypto

Everyone enters the cryptocurrency business in order to gain money, but not everyone succeeds in doing so. A large number of individuals either abandon up along the road or lose money as a result of their lack of understanding of how to generate money using cryptocurrencies. As of this writing, the cryptocurrency business is still in its phase of growth. As the value of crypto-assets rises, more individuals are attracted to the business as a result. These newbies are always attempting to find out how to earn money using cryptocurrencies, but not all of them succeed. The good news is that there are several avenues for earning money using cryptocurrencies available. From 2011 to the present, there has been constant rise in the amount of developer engagement, social media activity, and the number of cryptocurrency-related start-ups launched. Yes, it is possible to generate money with cryptocurrencies. Most crypto assets are high-risk due to their inherent volatility, and some need specific subject knowledge or experience to trade successfully.

Keep in mind that this industry is always changing. There isn't a single second that passes by without a deal being completed. With so many currency and fiat pairings to choose from, trading may easily become a full-time job for some.

What to avoid

Investing in the appropriate cryptocurrency at the right moment requires a certain amount of luck, but it also requires knowledge and accuracy. Only those that constantly improve their investing strategies, one error after another, will be able to continually outperform the majority. There are many typical blunders that one should avoid while investing in the very volatile cryptocurrency market. These include:

Unless you grasp the fundamentals of the technology, you will be at danger on the road ahead. You will lose out on significant chances unless you get the ability to evaluate initiatives for yourself. Some investors, mainly newcomers, want to make 20 transactions every day, which is a lot for them. This is quite risky. At the end of the day, many of them lose money due to fees or because they make terrible transactions and then trade more to make up for lost time. The fact is that there aren't 20 excellent trading chances available every day of the week. Excessive trading results in weak decision-making abilities. Overtrading also raises the amount of tax that you owe. Cryptocurrencies are not the same as equities or bonds. You do not own any stock in the firm and do not get any dividends. If a company issues a cryptocurrency, it is extremely likely that it will profit from the cryptocurrency or will be bought, with no benefit to you.

Even if a company is doing really well, the value of its currency might decrease. Don't chase after cheap coins while harboring fantasies of Lambos and private aircrafts. A large number of ignorant investors in the cryptocurrency market purchase low-priced coins because they believe they have a better chance of making large profits. This is a very frequent snare. There are several elements that influence the price of a coin, including two key ones: the number of coins in circulation and the worth of the currency in the actual world. Don't put all of your eggs in one basket, no matter how tempting it may seem. Investment in several assets is something that every competent investor does to hedge or shield his or her risk. It's a good idea to have at least 5 cryptocurrencies in your portfolio. A large number of investors are impatient and 'cut their losses' too soon as a result of their emotions. The cryptocurrency market is characterized by cycles, in which values increase and decrease dramatically over a short period of time. If you purchase at a high price, you will have to wait through a full new market cycle in order to make money — which means a new bear market followed by a new bull market — which might take several months to more than a year. As a result, never, ever put money at risk that you can't afford to lose in order to make money!

Crypto Strategies

In this chapter, we will discuss the most common strategies for investing in coins. These methods will serve as the basis for future tactics that you will undoubtedly get used to as you're investing and trading talents develop and evolve.

Pick the right coin for you

Picking out coins to invest in is not easy, but one of the most important parts of investing. For novice investors it's often easiest to pick coins based on other people (i.e., following the crowd). However, there are plenty of ways to research new coins and tokens that haven't yet entered the mainstream, taking into account some of the following factors:

Industry: What is the industry that this coin will be used in? Is it a growing market, or is it going to fall away soon? Industry changes can have a big impact on whether a coin will rise or fall. For example, though most coins do not survive, some coins work with specific industries like pharmaceuticals or finance.

Team: Who are the people behind the coin? Are they trustworthy and smart? Also, their history in crypto is important to go further with your due diligence of them. If they've been involved in previous coins that have fallen apart, it's probably not a good idea to invest in them. For example, if you're considering seeing what the team behind your coin is like, take a quick look at profiles on social media.

Technology: What kind of technology will the coin use? Is it new or is it outdated? If it's new, will the technology stay unaltered throughout the years ahead? Will this coin be able to expand and grow with time, or will its technology be obsolete in a few months (or even weeks)?

Partnerships: Who can benefit from using your coin? Will it be able to work with other coins and technologies? The more partnerships the better, as the value of a coin rests on its uses and applications.

Tokens: Is your coin an ERC-20 token or is it its own blockchain (or both)? Investors like tokens since they're easier to store and trade than actual cryptocurrencies (some of them aren't even actual cryptocurrencies), but they can also be riskier.

Whitepaper: Does the coin have a whitepaper (or some other form of documentation) for investors? Is it easy to understand or is it like reading Greek? Investors should not only look at what the technology does, but how it works and what it does.

Of course, there are many other factors to consider like how much the coin is worth and whether or not it can keep growing in value (the price of a new coin should ideally rise after its launch). These might be some things that you want to look at when you're evaluating new coins for investment purposes. So always take So always take a look before you put your money up.

In short, knowing what factors to consider when looking at coins can help you to avoid potential pitfalls and make good investment decisions. Just remember that the list above is not complete or exhaustive - there are other things that might be important to take into account while researching a coin.

Whenever you are looking to invest in a new coin, always do your research first, read reviews/feedback from other investors, see what people are saying on social media about the coin etc. Usually, you won't find large groups of investors who are selling because it's expected to rise in price. If you see a lot of red flags stay away from the coin, there is probably something wrong with it.

Now let's talk about some more practical strategies investors can use.

Grow your profits and cut your losses

In reality, the natural instinct of new traders is to sell winners as soon as they are profitable in order to protect their gains. While doing so, people hold onto losers not simply to prevent losses, but also in the belief that the currency would someday rise in value. Because it's painful to be proven incorrect. Nonetheless, this is a very regular circumstance that is well-described by the trading adage "keep wins for longer and sell losers quicker," which is well-known in the trading industry. That is to say, you should bear in mind that trading, and cryptocurrency trading in particular, is an area in which all of your fundamental impulses are often counterintuitive, so you should be aware of this before entering the market. Make a better decision and build your trading strategy on making profits over a longer period of time rather than gaining profit from a single transaction. Approach crypto trading in the same way you would any other profession. It's a time-consuming and frustrating procedure at times that might take some time to complete successfully. In the end you will be awarded with monetary compensation.

That is a proven truth. Furthermore, it is recommended that you do not invest an amount that would negatively impact your financial situation at once, at least in the first year of your investment. In most cases, an amount equal to 5 percent of your capital is sufficient. The reason why you need a trading strategy is precisely so that you can limit your losses. You may get the impression that you need to close or reopen a certain order. The weather is pleasant, you are fortunate, and the trend is upward. But keep in mind that transactions that aren't on your plan aren't there for no apparent reason. This is the non-anxious version of yourself telling you to take a break and manage your risks before you go insane. Create a strategy that is tailored to your trading style and account size so that you will know when it is appropriate to exit a trade if the deal goes south. Why would you give up while you're feeling fortunate? Because your notebook specifically said that you should. Essentially, the goal is straightforward: to premeditate enough leeway for the price to wriggle in your favor before the trend begins moving against you, and to exit as soon as the trend starts moving against you. You will have more time to seek for other options as a result of this. While developing your cryptocurrency trading strategy, bear in mind that the entry and exit points, which you should have documented in your diary in advance, are critical in determining your levels on the upside and downside of the market. This gradually brings us to the topic of how much you're willing to put your money at danger. However, having a strategy meticulously stated on a piece of paper in a calm state of mind can assist you in maintaining discipline when your hair is on fire, which is something that occurs fairly often in the process of cryptocurrency trading.

Following on from the last section, you may have surmised that there are a number of tools available that may assist you in calculating the risks associated with your trading activities. But let's start with what you want to achieve. Your objective is straightforward. A single transaction should not have a significant influence on your account balance, even if the deal results in a profit — good traders generate consistent profits over time. It occurs as a result of their setting realistic objectives and maintaining a cautious approach that involves a number of factors. First and first, you should trade in the direction of a trend, and second, you should abandon the trade as soon as you discover clear proof that the trade is terrible. In fact, it is human instinct to hope that things will improve when things go wrong, which may pose a concern in this case. In addition, it is beneficial to avoid margin trading and to be optimistic on cryptocurrency that is essentially sound. In addition, you have the option of downsizing your holdings and receiving a lesser proportion of each coin, which brings us to the following topic, which is the diversification of your investment portfolio. By including assets that have little correlation with one another, you may reduce the likelihood of portfolio risk. For example, you may combine fresh cryptocurrencies with well-established stablecoins, or combine it with a small amount of Bitcoin and certain forked projects. Don't forget to diversify your investments depending on growth pace, market capitalization, and level of maturity.

Follow the trend

A good investment strategy is to follow the trend on the way up and down. You are basically following the superior trend to maximize your profit. This strategy is simple but hard to execute. You should remain cool in times of high volatility because your chance to make money goes up when there are huge swings in the market. If you panic every time the market swings, it will be hard to stay cool and make money.

What's most important is that you don't lose your money or miss opportunities by trying to pick a perfect entry or exit point. This approach might help you minimize the risks and is a good strategy for beginners.

Do not follow the crowd blindly

Many people lose money because they buy what everyone is buying and selling when everyone else is selling. A lot of new cryptocurrency investors buy Dogecoin, Shiba Inu or Tron without any research simply because it's on all the other crypto websites as well as most news articles. Some of these investors might even buy the coin really early on when it's still cheap, but they are actually doing something very risky. When new projects get hyped up and the whole market rises, then it is important to know that all cryptocurrencies follow suit. This will not be like this forever and you should try not to follow the crowd blindly, but do some research first.

Know the basics for trading

Cryptocurrencies, the stock market or anything else that can fluctuate in price and be traded with a chart is where it is recommended that traders begin their trading journey by gaining a basic understanding of what a trend line is, how to trade with trendlines, and what support and resistance levels are. You need to know about reading a chart, creating a trend line, as well as understanding support and resistance lines and how to trade cryptocurrencies. You should feel secure enough to design your own trend line trading technique by the time you finish it.

Build a diversified crypto portfolio

Create a diversified portfolio to minimize risk while maximizing your potential. There are two types of portfolios: Hold only cryptocurrencies or hold both cryptocurrency and traditional.

A very good diversified portfolio will consist of both cryptocurrencies and traditional assets. The use of both allows you to hedge against volatility in the price of cryptocurrency, while increasing your chances at gaining profits. This is because when one asset's value decreases, another increases - since they are different.

If you want to stay in the crypto space, start by buying bitcoins or Ethereum, then purchase other cryptos that are valuable and interesting, but remember to research the project well before you invest. As a rule of thumb each asset should be around 5% of your total investment. That way, even if one coin went to zero, the other assets would help you recoup your losses. Over the year you might still be very profitable. It's important not to chain yourself to just bitcoin. There are other coins that offer great value and can substitute for BTC in your portfolio if necessary.

When to sell

The choice regarding whether to sell a financial investment is not unique to cryptocurrencies or blockchain technology. Any investor who wants to make a profit must confront this obstacle. If you think about equities during the dotcom boom, you can draw some useful parallels that can help you make better decisions concerning cryptocurrencies. The 1990s saw a large number of individuals invest in internet-related firms. Individuals who possessed dotcom firm stocks were faced with the decision of whether to keep or sell their investments as the value of these equities increased. It was inevitable that the bubble would burst. The majority of those that hung onto their dotcom stocks and did not sell anything suffered a significant loss. Profits were made by those who sold, though. They were able to cash out. Despite the fact that they sold before their separate assets reached their peak value, they still made a significant amount of money. Both instances demonstrate the importance of understanding one's own personal goals and expectations.

When it comes to investing, investors always want to make the most money possible, thus a better guideline is to ask yourself: What am I prepared to lose? The capacity to establish expectations about how much risk you can tolerate in the turbulent cryptocurrency markets may be achieved by developing an investing strategy that is led by your ability to absorb losses. What kind of returns would you want to see from investing in the cryptocurrency market? Is a 5% increase in profits over the period of 30 days sufficient? Are you wanting to increase the value of your investment by doubling it? Questionnaires like this one may help you better understand your objectives and goals, as well as determine how much time you would want to devote to the markets on any given day. The volatility that is now inherent in cryptocurrencies causes day traders to spend their waking hours staring at the computer, attempting to capitalize on profits as they come in while simultaneously attempting to offset losses as they go out. Understanding how cryptocurrency exchanges operate, as well as the rate at which currencies rise and fall, can provide you with a better understanding of what to anticipate. There are a variety of ideas that you may use to assist you in making selections regarding establishing plans for when you want to sell a certain currency in the future.

One method of taking a more cautious approach to crypto trading is to anticipate keeping your money for a longer length of time (hold). Allowing yourself the time to observe profits over time may help you reduce your exposure while increasing your chances of making money in the long run, especially in the cryptocurrency markets, which are notoriously volatile. As soon as you have worked out how the markets function and believe you are ready to begin trading, you will need to establish some goals for yourself, devise a trading plan, and follow through with it.

Do not fight the whales

The next thing you might want to look at are what are called "whales". These are big-time investors who hold a lot of coins that can drive up or down the price of a coin. When you see someone with 100,000+ coins, then it's probably the same person moving the price up or down using their holdings (and they're definitely not doing something illegal). Don't try to compete against these big players - try to follow them instead.

For example, if someone has majority control over a cryptocurrency, then they're able to alter the blockchain in their favor - usually by means of modifying transaction times, fees or other important details. And while you might think that it's morally wrong for them to do so, there isn't much you could do about it.

A whale is probably someone with around 500+ BTC (Bitcoin) worth of holdings, though it could be less depending on the market. If you see someone who has more coins than most people combined, then there's a big chance they're driving the prices up or down with their own holdings. Just follow them instead of trying to compete against them - they'll usually do what's best for their own investment in the long run.

One last thing about whales is to be careful when they're getting out of a coin. Just like how it's bad for them if the market tanks, they're going to want to get rid of their holdings while the price is still high. So, whenever you see a big player selling off their coins, then there's a good chance that it's going to go down in the near future.

What does HODL mean? Long term investment

Suppose you're going through social media and you come across someone who is "HODLING" or who is encouraging someone else to "HODL." Confused? Actually, it is not misspelled. HODL is a cryptocurrency-related slang term that refers to the misspelt version of the word "hold." Maintaining your crypto assets over a lengthy period of time, even during periods of extreme market volatility, is what this term alludes to. When a cryptocurrency decreases substantially in value or climbs in value to the point that it is very lucrative to sell, the term "Hold" is used to persuade individuals to refrain from selling hastily. HOLD ON FOR DEAR LIFE" is an abbreviation that may also be used to refer to a situation in which one must hold on for dear life. In different cryptocurrency forums and social media circles, you'll often come across the word "blockchain." In other cases, influencers even push their followers to "hold" different crypto-tokens as part of a long-term investment plan.

When discussing the buy-and-hold strategy, the term "hold" has been in use for a very long time in finance. In this investment approach, you purchase a financial item and retain it for an unlimited amount of time after making the purchase. An investor should not be misled by short-term market swings and should instead have a long-term perspective, according to this viewpoint: Perhaps the most significant reason why "hold" has become such a well-known expression is the overall volatility of cryptocurrency pricing. Even somewhat stable cryptocurrencies such as Bitcoin and Ethereum, along as many other cryptocurrencies, are subject to extreme market volatility on a regular basis. The value of these tokens may drop by 100 percent in a single month and then climb by 300 percent in the next few months, depending on the market conditions. In addition, the movements of whales have a significant impact on cryptocurrency values (a term for people or organizations that hold a very large amount of a particular token). One whale selling a specific token has the potential to completely devastate its market value.

Coin Staking

Staking is a way to get rewarded for locking up your coins in a wallet. You can keep the staking coins in that wallet and let it stake, or you can have it lend them to a master node who recompense you with more coin for doing this.

Staking is good for passive income. All you have to do is buy the coin and let it sit in a wallet. This works well for coins that have high expected returns. Some coins even have Master nodes which pay you dividends for running them. Basically, it's earning interest on top of increasing value of your own portfolio. The best part is that you don't need to do anything else, but hold the coin in your online wallet like you would do when buying and holding.

Crypto day trading

Although this is a popular topic, I would probably not recommend it for you. You can't make a living on crypto day trading because of the low volume, high volatility and high commissions. What's the point of trading and earning small percent on your trade if you have to pay huge commissions? Don't even talk about the spread, which is sometimes astronomical for small trades.

But since this topic is so popular, I would like to give some advice: If you plan on getting active in trading (because you have enough money to do so), don't just jump into the deep end and begin right away. Start with a demo account and learn how to trade first. You will not earn money, but also not lose anything. See if your plans work in reality.

A lot of new investors try their luck at this because it's easy money, right? Maybe not. It takes a lot of time and research to day trade correctly and even then; you can't guarantee success.

Special Deals

The use of cryptocurrencies may be used to generate income in a variety of methods, some of which need you to spend nothing more than your time and efforts. It is also possible to make money with cryptocurrencies by participating in bonus/airdrop deals, which do not need any investment on your part. Simply participating in an airdrop or bounty program of a cryptocurrency and completing some simple chores is all that is required to receive some free or extra coins in exchange. Additionally, by investing in a cryptocurrency during an initial coin offering (ICO) or token sale period, you may receive additional tokens, since new projects often provide bonus tokens to early investors.

Basics of Crypto Analysis

To be successful at investing or trading in cryptocurrencies, you need to know and understand the basics. Technical analysis is a tool that helps investors predict what will happen with a coin's price in the future by taking into account historic data such as daily average percentage changes, highs and lows. Investors use this information to weigh their investment decisions and plan out future strategies.

Financial charts are used to track current and past market activity, analyze past trends, determine support or resistance levels, measure momentum, provide general trading signals, identify breakouts, chart patterns, calculate the probability of potential price movements.

Using technical analysis for crypto is not much different from traditional investing with stocks. You need to know what are the daily percentage changes in price, how high or low a coin has reached in the past and stay updated with news related to the crypto market. It is also crucial to understand trends in order to predict what might happen next.

Why learn to read charts

If you want to go into cryptocurrency trading, learning how to interpret crypto charts is a must-have ability. Even yet, studying technical analysis and all of the language that goes with it may be difficult for those who are just getting started. This is why we've put up this guide to make your trip a little easier.

To have a better understanding of technical analysis, it is necessary to be familiar with the Dow Theory (stock market). Let's take a look at it and try to match it with the crypto market. The following are the key concepts that underpin it: During the price process, the market takes everything into account. Currently available, historical, and forthcoming information has already been included into the value of current asset values. Several aspects, including present, historical, and future demand, as well as any potential restrictions that may have an influence on the market, are taken into account.

The swings of the market are not completely random. They are more likely than not to follow patterns, which may be long-term or short-term in nature. Market analysts are more concerned with the price of an asset than they are with each and every element that influences the its price movement. History has a tendency to repeat itself. Market behavior may be predicted as a result of this phenomenon, since traders all respond similarly when faced with a given kind of pattern. The principal movement is referred to as the "main movement," which is a big trend that may continue anywhere from a few months to many years. It may be either bullish or bearish in nature. Then there is the medium swing, which is a secondary or intermediate response that may last anywhere from ten days to three months in duration. On average, it retraces between 33 percent and 66 percent of the primary price shift since the last medium swing or the beginning of the major movement. Finally, we have the brief swing or small movement, which may last anywhere from a few hours to a month or more depending on market speculation. These three movements may occur at the same time, for example, a daily minor movement followed by a bearish secondary response followed by a bullish primary movement can occur at the same time.

When new information becomes available, the market integrates it as soon as it is made public. Immediately upon the publication of this news, the price of the asset changes in order to reflect the new information. The price represents the total of all of the hopes, concerns, and expectations expressed by all of the players in the market. Variations in interest rates as well as earnings predictions and revenue projections, as well as important elections and product developments, are all included into the market price.

Of course, the crypto market is a bit different, but there are also many similarities. And many investors will use the available tools for the crypto market as well, which has a heavy influence on their behavior and will in conclusion influence the market.

Having this in mind, let us now investigate what technical analysis is all about. An instrument or approach used to forecast the likely future price movement of a currency pair, cryptocurrency pair, or a stock is known as technical analysis. It may be a creative and dynamic process that allows you to obtain a highly detailed understanding of the industry.

Technical analysis for beginners

For Crypto, which is mostly unregulated and therefore a lot harder to analyze, technical analysis is very important. Since there are real investors using it for their investments, you can use the information they generate to make your own strategy. In other words: the more people use technical analysis in crypto, the better our strategies get because we all learn from each other with time.

Technical analysis is the evaluation of price and volume data and trying to predict future movements based on that. There are several ways to do technical analysis. Fundamental analysis, as opposed to technical analysis, is primarily concerned with determining if a coin is overvalued or undervalued in the first place.

The most common way of technical analysis is using candles, where you look at how candles react during different times and use their height and color (open & close) as inputs for your prediction. You can start off with very basic tools, but I personally recommend Tradingview. It's cheap and has many different tools for free.

Other ways to do technical analysis is using indicators such as the Relative Strength Index (RSI), Stochastic Oscillator, Moving Average Convergence Divergence (MACD) and many more. I won't go through the different indicators in detail since this will fill another book, but if you're interested in advanced technical analysis, I recommend learning about them and finding what works for you.

The simplest way to do technical analysis is just looking at the chart. You can add or remove indicators that fit your strategy and predict price movements based on it. All these indicators work with different time frames, but all of them use the same principle: The specific value or values calculated from one or several previous values.

When it comes to price, the market takes everything into account. Currently available, prior, and upcoming information has already been factored into the value of current asset prices. In the case of Bitcoin and cryptocurrency, this would include a variety of variables such as current, past, and future demand, as well as any regulations that may have an impact on the cryptocurrency market. A response to all of the current details, which include the expectations and knowledge of each coin traded on the market, the current price is determined. Technicians' analyses what the price is telling them about the state of the market in order to make calculated and wise predictions about future pricing.

The change of prices is not arbitrary. Rather, they tend to follow trends, which can be either long-term or short-term in nature. Following the formation of a trend by a coin, it is likely that the coin will follow that trend in order to oppose it. Technical analysts attempt to uncover and benefit from trends via the use of technical analysis.

'What' is more important than 'Why' in this situation. Technicians are more concerned with the price of a coin than they are with the variables that cause the coin's price to fluctuate. Despite the fact that a variety of factors could have influenced the price of a coin to move in a particular direction, technicians confidently examine supply and demand.

History has a tendency to repeat itself. It is feasible to forecast the psychology of the market. When traders are presented with similar stimuli, they can sometimes react in the same way.

Trend lines

When it comes to cryptocurrency trading, trend lines, or the normal direction that a coin is travelling in, may be quite advantageous. It should be noted that distinguishing between these patterns might be more difficult stated than done. Cryptocurrency assets may be quite volatile, and looking at a Bitcoin or cryptocurrency price movement chart will almost certainly display a series of highs and lows that create a linear pattern over time. When considering the volatility of the market, technical analysts recognize that they may ignore it and identify an upward trend when they observe a series of higher highs, and that they can do the same when they see a series of lower lows. Additional trends that travel sideways exist, and a coin does not move considerably in either direction when these trends occur. Traders should keep in mind that trends may manifest themselves in a variety of ways, including intermediate, long, and short-term trend lines.

Supports and resistances

In the same way that there are trend lines, there are also horizontal lines that indicate levels of support and resistance. It is possible to make inferences about the present supply and demand of the currency by recognizing the values of these levels. The presence of a significant number of traders who are eager to acquire the coin (a strong demand) indicates that the currency is priced cheap at this level, and as a result, those traders will want to purchase the currency at that price when it reaches support. The creation of a "floor" of purchasers occurs when the coin's value approaches that threshold. The high demand generally brings the downward trend to a halt, and in some cases even transforms the momentum to an upward trend.

A level of resistance is the polar opposite of a level of supply — it is a zone in which a big number of sellers set their orders to walk away with profit, establishing a vast supply zone. Every time the coin gets close to that "ceiling," it runs into the huge supply and is forced to reverse course. Trade-offs between support and resistance levels are often seen, with traders tending to accumulate on support lines while selling near resistance levels. This generally occurs when a lateral movement is seen as a potential opportunity. So, what exactly occurs when a resistance or support level is broken through? There is a significant likelihood that this is an indication that is bolstering the current upward or downward trend. Further confirmation of the trend is acquired when the resistance level becomes the support level, and when the support level is challenged from above immediately after the breakout. False breakouts occur when a breakout occurs, but the trend does not shift as a result of the breakout. As a result, we must use other indications, such as trade volume, to determine the direction of the trend.

In detail, support is a price level at which a downturn is predicted to come to a stop owing to a concentration of demand or purchasing activity. Whenever the value of assets or securities declines, there is a rise in demand for those assets or securities, which results in the formation of the support line. However, during times of price growth, resistance zones form as a result of the selling interest that occurs. Identifying areas of support and resistance can help traders identify potential entry and exit points because, when a price reaches one of these levels of support or resistance, it will do one of two things: either bounce back away from the level of support or resistance, or violate the price level and continue in its direction, until it reaches the next level of support or resistance. It is believed that support and resistance zones will not be breached, which influences the timing of certain transactions. traders may "bet" on price movement and immediately assess whether they are accurate, regardless of whether the price is stopped by or breaks through a support or resistance level. Even if the price swings in the incorrect direction, the trade may be terminated with just a little loss if the trend continues.

However, if the price swings in the proper direction, the move might be significant. Even the most experienced traders can tell you anecdotes about how certain price levels tend to deter traders from moving the price of an underlying asset in a certain direction, despite their best efforts. Because resistance levels signify locations where a rally runs out of steam, resistance levels are sometimes referred to as ceilings.

Moving Averages

Moving averages are another technical analysis technique for crypto currencies, as well as for technical analysis in general, that may be used to facilitate the identification of trends. A moving average is calculated by using the average price of a coin over a certain period of time as its basis. Example: A moving average for any particular day will be generated based on the price of a coin over the preceding 20 trading days in order to arrive at that day's moving average. A line is formed by connecting all of the moving averages. Another notable indicator is the exponential moving average (EMA), which is a moving average that gives greater weight in its computation to the price values of the most recent few days than the price values of the prior days. To provide an example, the calculation coefficient of the final five trading days of the EMA 15 days will be twice as high as that of the prior ten. A real-world illustration may be seen in the following graph: If a 10-day moving average crosses over a 30-day moving average, it might indicate the beginning of a bullish trend.

Fundamentals

In order to comprehend cryptocurrencies, investors need first recollect the basic ideas of monetary institutions: They are primarily used as units of measurement, as well as repositories of value and as trade mediums. Crypto tokens and coins often exhibit these three properties of traditional money. However, as an investor, I recommend that you assess whether or not these features are just a result of the goal that the asset's designers encoded into its software code before making a cryptocurrency investment. It is essential to have a thorough grasp of the assets and technology involved in cryptocurrency trading before even considering getting into the business of cryptocurrency trading. Countless different cryptocurrencies have sprung from the soil that Bitcoin has provided. As a result, it is important to first comprehend the asset that served as the basis around which the crypto sector was built. When it comes to building wealth in the cryptocurrency economy, it is important to understand the absolute fundamentals of cryptocurrency trading.

For your coin or token of choice, answer these questions:

- What specific problem that it aims to solve?
- Who are its competitors?
- Who are project supporters?
- How much volume is on the exchange you want to trade on?
- Is there a total supply of coins or only a circulating supply?
- What is the total market cap for all coins and tokens combined?
- Are there any future plans to increase demand for this coin/token?
- Is the coin/token being traded against other cryptocurrencies or fiat currencies?
- How stable is the market price for this coin/token?

Remember, cryptocurrencies are an extremely volatile asset class that often have multiple different values at the same time. It is important to understand precisely what you are investing in before putting any money down.

Things to look out for: Value, Market cap & dilution

The entire value of all of the coins that have been minted, is known as the market capitalization (or market cap). The market capitalization of a cryptocurrency is derived by multiplying the total number of coins that have been minted by the current price of a single coin.

If the market cap increases by creating tokens out of thin air, this is known as dilution. This is used to describe the reduction in value of an asset that occurs as a result of the creation of additional units of that asset. Dilution is the result of inflation caused by an increase in supply. Your individual share of the whole market of this asset is being reduced, thus the value of your investment goes down a little bit. It is a common practice that the monetary policy of a cryptocurrency project aims to be anti-dilutive, but some projects are printing like the FED does in the FIAT world.

When it comes to market capitalization, one way to look about it is as an approximate indicator of how stable an asset is likely to be. As with a larger ship, however, a cryptocurrency with a lot greater market capitalization is more likely to be a more stable investment than one with a much lower market capitalization, in the same way that a larger ship can safely traverse severe weather. Smaller market capitalization digital currencies, on the other hand, are more sensitive to the vagaries of the market, with the potential for either massive profits or spectacular losses after their devaluation or inflation. If a project with a big market cap would collapse however, it would more likely take the whole market down with it.

Market cycles

Market cycles are an unavoidable part of each market's life cycle. However, since the crypto market moves at such a rapid pace, understanding market cycles is particularly crucial. After taking all into consideration, let's go through the most basic explanation of what a market cycle is. A market cycle is defined as the time span between a high and a low, as well as the phases in between those two extremes.

Smart money, institutional investors, early adopters, and others amass crypto at a low price point. They accumulate during a lower period that looks like anger and depression to those who held from the last peak. When the market is on the rise, more and more small investors enter in, causing a period of exuberance. As the market grows and more investors join in, institutional investors start selling. At this stage we usually see a high volume on exchanges and the price is inflated beyond reality. Once the best time to sell has passed and prices have exploded, big players start selling cryptocurrencies in large quantities. When panic sets in and the market crashes, those who got in early make up most of the profits. This is why it's generally a good idea to not day-trade or speculate on bitcoin prices (unless you're swimming in more money than you know what to do with) as this will distort market cycles and will cause people to lose money. Those who invested at the bottom and held through the lows as well as the highs, however, tend to do very well. It's those who panic sell that lose money in a bear market and those who pump that become poor.

Understanding market cycles is one of the most important things you can learn if you want understand how to invest properly. By understanding this principle, you will better understand how the cycle works.

Crypto and the rest of the world

Crypto is becoming more and more popular, leading to more and more things that need to be taken care of. Your government will probably want to see its share via taxes. You need to choose the right platform to buy and sell. You will be tempted by scammers - better learn what you're up against (and how to avoid it). It's especially hard for beginners because of all the information, but also the bad advice that exists out there.

Taxes on Crypto

A lot of individuals that got into cryptocurrencies (whether via mining or investing) probably didn't even thought about the tax ramifications of their investments before the 2017 crypto craze. However, as bitcoin investment has grown more common, the taxes standards governing it have stolen the spotlight. Throughout this chapter, I will go through the fundamentals of cryptocurrency taxes. As a consequence of your investment in all of the high-priced equipment discussed in previous chapters and your receipt of crypto mining earnings, you may be regarded as a cryptocurrency company owner. You are theoretically being compensated in cryptos for your commercial activity, and as a result, you are liable to income taxation by the Internal Revenue Service. It goes without saying that if you work for a company that pays you in cryptocurrency, you'll be liable to income tax as well.

US

Creating a corporation or a corporate entity around your mining operations rather than mining as a self-employed person may result in a lower tax rate if you live in the United States. You are able to take advantage of the tax reductions available to company owners when they spend money on business-related expenses, as well as benefit from lower tax rates than those applicable to individuals. Have you gotten your hands on that high-end PC for Bitcoin mining? You may deduct it from your company profits and reduce your taxable earnings. It is the same as the capital gains tax rate for federal income taxes when it comes to bitcoin. In 2021, the rate for short-term capital gains will vary from 10-37 percent, while the rate for long-term capital gains will range from 0 to 20 percent.

According to the Internal Revenue Service, crypto-asset gains are determined based on two factors: your income and the length of time you have had the coin (holding period). A capital asset's holding period starts on the day after it is purchased or a bitcoin transaction is completed and ends on the day it is traded, sold, or otherwise distributed. Short-term capital gains and long-term capital gains are two types of capital gains that may be recognized. You will be liable to ordinary income tax on your cryptocurrency coins if you retain them for fewer than 365 days, and you will be subject to short-term capital gains tax if you hold them for more than 365 days.

UK

While cryptocurrency is a relatively new asset, its regulations are still being established. There are several misunderstandings about crypto asset taxation in the United Kingdom, one of which is that they are outside the scope of UK tax because they are considered a "winner" similar to gambling or playing the lottery. That is incorrect. The HMRC does not consider crypto assets to be money, whether exchange tokens, utility tokens, or security tokens. It is also dependent on how the tokens are used when it comes to taxing them. In the United Kingdom, any profits over £12,300 are taxed.

Germany

In Germany, cryptocurrency is regarded as a private asset, which means it is subject to individual income tax rather than capital gains tax, as is the case in other countries. The most important thing to understand is that Germany only taxes cryptocurrency if it is sold within the same year that it was purchased. As a result, although Germany taxes some crypto-related activities, including as short-term trading, mining, and staking, its crypto-related tax policies are far more permissive than those in other nations. This is due to the fact that bitcoin and other cryptocurrencies are not considered property under German tax laws. In its place, Bitcoin is categorized as an 'other asset,' and selling it is considered a 'private disposition.' Because the private sale of assets in Germany is tax-favored, it is critical to understand the differences. Following a one-year holding period, crypto profits are totally tax-free in Germany since they are considered a "private sale." Furthermore, gains from cryptocurrency sales up to 600€ per calendar year are exempt from taxation. The usage of cryptocurrencies for long-term financial investment and the absence of frequent relocation of these assets allow crypto traders in Germany to make tax-free income.

Applicability in Society

Cryptocurrency has come a long way since its appearance in 2009 with the creation of Bitcoin. Bitcoin is seen as a groundbreaking invention by some. Others see it as a passing tidal wave that will soon pass. However, for some, Bitcoin is a digital money that will be around for a long time. Some individuals are now questioning how Bitcoin will help society as a whole.

What kind of contribution do you think cryptocurrencies will make to the world? Is it possible for Bitcoin to make administrative and financial tasks easier?

If crypto is utilized correctly, it has the potential to benefit mankind in a variety of ways. Since infancy, the majority of people have understood the significance of fiat money. Money is more than just a fixed number of banknotes and coins that people use as a regular payment method; it is also the root of administrative and financial matters.

The problem is that fiat money can be manipulated or misused, especially by the state's governments. Cryptocurrencies like Bitcoin were born with the goal to eliminate this situation. Who doesn't want more freedom? The freedom to manage your own transactions without having any middleman involved; it is a dream for most.

The adoption of crypto as a method of payment for services or goods by the general public is still in the early stages, but it is growing exponentially. If more and more people start using crypto, it can change the world.

Bitcoin and other cryptocurrencies have long been spoken about and debated, but they're just now coming to light as financial instruments that can be used by people other than crypto-enthusiasts and are helpful to a wider range of people. In addition to providing easier access to finance and financial services, cryptocurrencies have great promise for promoting social and economic development around the globe, particularly in poor nations. Blockchain technology, in general, and bitcoin in particular, have a very utilitarian, but also disruptive, characteristic, which has gradually, but steadily, begun to interfere with the way the existing financial system operates.

There is already a whole business established around cryptocurrencies, and it is controlled by organizations tasked with overseeing all of the digital currency transactions that take place all over the globe, including the United States. The velocity at which the cryptocurrency sector is developing is unprecedented, as seen by the wealth of early adopters who became millionaires overnight and discovered new avenues for financial growth. Bitcoin, the most well-known of these cryptocurrencies, has already enabled many individuals and businesses to expand and prosper, and many of these individuals and businesses depend on trading as a source of revenue. Slowly but steadily, the economy is evolving to meet these requirements, and cryptocurrencies have a tremendous deal of promise in fulfilling them.

Popular Trading Apps & Platforms

If you want to start, you need to transfer funds to a crypto trading platform by using your traditional currency.

Here is a list of popular cryptocurrency exchanges, as well as well-known cryptocurrency investment and trading platforms. Make your own research as there are countless quickly evolving platforms and the information here might be out of date when you are reading this.

Whatever platform you choose, do not rush and make sure that it is possible to get your funds back out. (Don't worry about the other way, they will most likely accept your money on the way in). As a rule of thumb, the bigger and the better established, the better are your chances. Always keep in mind what country your exchange is based in, since this might be a big deal. Ever wanted to fly to the Cayman Islands to try to get your money back?

Coinbase

Coinbase has established itself as the dominant popular cryptocurrency, serving as a standard on-ramp for new crypto investors. Even when trading on other platforms, many start by changing their fiat money on Coinbase and transfer Ethereum or Bitcoin to the exchange wanting to trade.

Coinbase is completely regulated and licensed in many countries and listed on the stock market.

Binance

The Binance exchange is based on the Cayman Islands. It is compatible with the majority of cryptocurrencies that are traded on exchanges worldwide. Trading on Binance is made possible via the use of a cryptocurrency wallet. Users may also earn interest or trade with cryptocurrencies using the exchange's supporting services.

Kraken

Kraken, situated in the US is a cryptocurrency exchange, allowing market players to trade many different cryptocurrencies. A variety of fiat currencies, including the United States dollar, Canadian dollar, euro, and the Japanese yen, are authorized to be used in the purchase and sale of cryptocurrencies by users.

FTX

FTX is based on the Bahamas after moving from Hong Kong. User can trade a wide spectrum of financial products and cryptocurrency.

eToro

A social trading and multi-asset brokerage firm based in Israel, eToro is focused on offering financial and copy trading services in financial markets including cryptocurrencies. The advantage of a one stop shop broker is that you have access to a variety of crypto assets, traditional stocks and financial products from one trading platform. Be careful when buying leveraged products since the odds are against you.

KuCoin

KuCoin is based in the Seychelles. In addition to allowing, you to buy, sell, and trade a wide variety of cryptocurrencies, Ku Coin is also a third-party exchange that offers a variety of services.

Bitfinex

Bitfinex is based on the British Virgin Islands. Despite still having large trading volume, it is known through the community for several incidents where customers money was lost. It is closely attached to the Tether stablecoin which has come under suspicion lately.

Safety: Avoid Crypto Scams & Tips on Security

After getting your feet wet in the digital crypto world, it probably doesn't take long for you to realize that there is a significant amount of danger associated with these transactions that have nothing to do with the market's volatility. Scams can be found anywhere on the internet, and the crypto is no exception. Be aware of the risks associated with investing in various crypto projects and exchange platforms when you are starting out. Consider the following examples of more prevalent scams, as well as suggestions for avoiding being a victim while you participate in the exciting future of cryptocurrencies.

Do your research

When researching digital cryptocurrency projects and startups, it is recommended that you ensure that they are blockchain-based, which implies that they keep precise transaction data, according to industry experts. Additionally, be certain that they have good business ideas that address real-world issues. Companies should clarify their digital currency liquidity policies as well as their initial coin offering (ICO) guidelines. There should be genuine individuals working behind the scenes of the company. If the business you're considering doesn't have some of these traits, you should consider your options even more thoroughly before making your final selection.

AI Crypto Trading Bots

I've yet to discover one that actually works and makes people rich who have no connection to the company behind it. This may well change with more sophisticated technology. Who knows?

Pump and Dump (P&D) schemes

This is probably the easiest way to make quick money in the crypto space, but I wouldn't count on people getting away with this forever. Market manipulation can end you up in prison in some cases, keep that in mind. A

P&D scheme is basically when a group of people buy into their own coins in order to drive the price up, and then dump their coins once the price reaches its peak. While it may seem like an easy way to get rich quickly, this is actually a pyramid scheme that will only lead to losses for most people involved.

You've probably encountered P&D schemes in your local fiat currency if you have friends or family who are into investing. When a penny stock company has its share prices rise by 200% or more in a short period of time, people might start to believe that it's about to grow exponentially and make them rich overnight. The early investors will heavily promote the company in order to drive up demand, and others will follow suit in order to make a quick buck. But the company has no real strategy, no use case and won't actually benefit from having more money. In short, it's not worth buying into. The price will crash as soon as the early investors leave and the promotion stops.

Unfortunately, P&D schemes are common in the crypto space. Some people may claim that they have found a new coin that's going to take off in a few months and will make them rich. They'll tell you about all the good things it has, how much the price went up in a short period of time and how they need to buy in now before it's too late. P&D schemes are scams and if you know what you're doing, then you'll be able to spot a P&D scheme from a mile away.

While this isn't going to happen all the time (if it did, there wouldn't actually be any coins left), you should also be careful of people using bots or other automated techniques in order to buy up a lot of coins at once. This can drive up the price artificially. If you're really interested in a coin, then it might be better to buy into it during its ICO instead of trying to time your buy with other people who are also looking for quick profits.

Also, do not try to drive up a coin's price by yourself. Morality aside, this is both illegal and bad for the crypto space in general. Everyone should have equal access to coins, no matter how much money they have.

Imposter Websites

Even if you are following a sound recommendation from someone with extensive knowledge, you may become a victim of identity theft if you accidentally visit a bogus website. There are a surprising number of websites that have been created to seem like legitimate start-up companies. Take caution if there is no little lock symbol next to the URL bar, or if the site address does not begin with "https." Even though the site you believe you're visiting seems to be similar to the one you think you're visiting, you may be led to a different platform for payment. For example, you could click on a link that seems to go to a real website, but the attackers have crafted a fake URL that contains the number '0' instead of the letter 'O'. To prevent this, make sure you put the URL into your browser exactly as it appears. Just to make sure, double-check it if you plan to make a big transaction.

Fake Mobile Apps

Another popular method used by fraudsters is via the distribution of fake applications that can be downloaded from the Google Play Store. Although most people can typically immediately identify and delete these fake applications, this does not rule out the possibility that some investors fall for them. While this is a larger danger for Android users, it is something that every investor should be aware of, even when using an Apple device for example. Are there any apparent misspellings in the material, or even in the name of the application itself? Is the branding unauthentic, for example, because of unusual coloration or an erroneous logo? Take notice of this and think twice before downloading.

Fake Tweets and Other Social Media Updates

There is no way to know whether or not you are following impersonator accounts if you are following celebrities and corporate leaders on social media. Similarly, harmful, impersonating bots are prevalent in the cryptocurrency world, where they are used to mislead investors. Offers made on social media sites such as Twitter or Facebook should not be taken seriously, particularly if the outcome seems to be unattainable. False accounts may be found anywhere. Anyone who asks for even a tiny quantity of your bitcoin on one of these networks will very certainly never be able to recover that money. Similarly, just because other people are responding to your offer does NOT mean those responses are genuine. You must use extreme caution.

Scamming Emails

Although some email seems to be from a respectable cryptocurrency company, proceed with caution before investing your digital currency in the organization's products or services. Is the email exactly the same as before, and is the logo and branding the same as well? Can you confirm that the email address in question is a valid one associated with the company? One of the reasons it's crucial to select a company that has actual people working for it is the opportunity to check on this. If you have any questions concerning an email, you should consult with someone who works there. And never, ever go to a website by clicking on a link in an email. Scammers often launch fictitious ICOs, or initial coin offerings, in order to defraud investors out of large sums of money. Don't be fooled by these phone email and website promotions. Take your time to thoroughly examine all of the information. Unfortunately, there are a variety of methods in which certain Internet users might take advantage of insecure computer systems in order to mine or steal digital money. Before you begin investing in cryptocurrencies, educate yourself on how to be safe and protect yourself in this rapidly evolving marketplace.

Tips for Safety

Hackers' digital fingerprints may be completely obliterated, so it may be impossible to follow down their work. Because virtual currencies are presently controlled by any government institution or central bank, investors have little legal recourse if their cryptocurrency account is hacked, according to the Securities and Exchange Commission. So, the next step in ensuring crypto security is to be aware of the precautions that must be taken. Learn all you can about cryptocurrency exchanges and perform considerable research before you spend a single dime. This kind of platform allows users to buy and trade digital currencies, but there are a number of different exchanges to choose from. Consider doing your research, reading reviews, and speaking with more experienced investors before making a final selection. If you acquire bitcoin, you must keep it somewhere safe. You may store it in a digital wallet or trade it on a cryptocurrency market. While there is a plethora of wallets available, each has its own set of benefits, technical requirements, and security features that must be considered. Just like you would with trades, you should do your homework on storage choices before making a decision. Online wallets are growing more popular, drawing the attention of cybercriminals and attracting the attention of hackers. To be on the safe side, crypto should be housed in offline or physical wallets, with just a tiny portion of their holdings held in an online wallet.

The actual wallet should be maintained in a secure location, such as a safe or a safety deposit box, to prevent theft. It is also a good idea to keep the private and public keys separate. Complex passwords and multifactor authentication should be used to protect both accounts whenever feasible. If you have more than one account, never use the same password for each one, particularly because bitcoin services are a common target for hackers.

Assume anything online will all be affected by a data breach at some time in the future. You may reduce your risk by using a unique, strong password for each account, ideally with two-factor verification and password rotation enabled. Investors should thoroughly study the security aspects of each platform before deciding which one to use in order to understand how their information will be protected. When it comes to storing crypto, companies who can be trusted should have implemented the most advanced security measures available, such as multi-factor authentication, SSL/TLS encryption, and air-gapped devices that are kept offline. Whatever cryptocurrency platforms you use, it's vital to have a secure password manager on hand so that you don't lose track of your passwords and account information.

Maintaining current with information and changes pertaining to cryptocurrency security, on the other hand, is typically the greatest choice when it comes to implementing the most effective precautions for remaining secure in the cryptocurrency world.

NFT

Non-fungible tokens (NFTs) seem to have popped out of the ether lately and are all over the internet. These digital assets, which range from art and music to tacos and toilet paper, are selling like 17th-century exotic Dutch tulips, with some fetching millions of dollars. But are NFTs worth the money—and the hype—that they command? Some analysts believe they are a bubble primed to burst, similar to the dotcom mania or the popularity of Beanie Babies. Others feel that non-financial institutions (NFTs) are here to stay and that they will transform the face of investment forever. Art, music, in-game products, and films are all examples of digital assets. The majority of them are purchased and sold online, typically in exchange for cryptocurrency, and they are generally encoded using the same underlying software as many other digital currencies. However, despite the fact that they have been present since 2014, NFTs are expanding in popularity due to the fact that they are becoming an increasingly popular method of purchasing and selling digital artwork. Aside from that, NFTs are usually unique, or at the very least one of a very limited runs, and they are identified by unique identification codes.

Online, anybody may examine individual images—or even the full collage of images—for no charge at any time. Ironically, individuals are prepared to pay millions of dollars on something that they could simply capture or download for free and retain ownership of the original object. Not only that, but it also has built-in authentication, which acts as a means of establishing evidence of ownership. It is nearly as valuable as the object itself to collectors for them to have those "digital bragging rights."

NFTs are tokens that may be used to indicate ownership of one-of-a-kind goods, such as artwork. The ability to tokenize items like as art, valuables, and even real estate is provided by them. At any one moment, they can only have one legitimate owner, and they're protected by the Ethereum blockchain, which means that no one can amend the record of ownership or create a new NFT by copying and pasting an existing one. NFT is an abbreviation for non-fungible token. Non-fungible is an economic word that may be used to a variety of items, including your furniture, a music file, or even your computer system. These objects are not interchangeable with other items due to the fact that they have distinguishing characteristics. Items that are fungible, on the other hand, may be traded since their worth, rather than their unique features, determines what they are. If, for example, Ethereum or dollars are fungible, this means that 1 ETH or $1 USD may be exchanged for another 1 ETH or $1 USD.

What is it (NFT vs. Crypto)?

Generally speaking, NFT are developed using the same kind of programming as cryptocurrencies, such as Bitcoin or Ethereum, but that is about where the similarities between them stop. Currency in the form of physical money and cryptocurrencies are both "fungible," which means that they may be traded or swapped with one another. They're also the same in terms of value: one dollar is always worth another dollar, and one Bitcoin is always worth another Bitcoin, and so on. Because of cryptocurrency's fungibility, it is a reliable method of performing transactions on the blockchain. NFTs, on the other hand, are unique. Each NFT is protected by a digital signature, which makes it impossible for them to be swapped for or equated with one another in any way (hence, non-fungible).

The blockchain, which is a distributed public ledger that records transactions, is where NFTs are stored. You're probably most acquainted with blockchain since it's the fundamental technique that enables cryptocurrencies like Bitcoin and Litecoin feasible. In particular, NFTs are commonly stored on the Ethereum blockchain, however they may be stored on other blockchains as well. In essence, NFTs are similar to actual collector's artefacts, except that they are digital. As a result, rather of receiving a real oil painting to display on his or her wall, the customer receives a digital copy. In addition, they are granted exclusive ownership rights. That's correct: NFTs can only have a single owner at a given moment. Because each NFT has a unique ID, it is simple to verify ownership and transfer tokens between different owners. It is possible for the owner or author to keep special information inside them.

Using an NFT's metadata, artists may sign their work by putting their signature in the file's information. Artists and content producers have a unique potential to monetize their work thanks to blockchain technology and non-fungible tokens (NFTs). When it comes to selling their artwork, artists no longer have to depend on galleries or auction houses. An NFT, may be sold directly to the customer by the artist and allows them to retain a larger portion of the revenues. Apart from that, artists have the option of programming royalties into their artwork so that they get a portion of revenues every time their work is sold to a new owner. This is a desirable feature since, in most cases, artists do not get any further income once their artwork has been sold.

Art isn't the only method to generate money with NFTs; there are other options as well. Brands such as Charmin and Taco Bell have auctioned off themed NFT paintings in order to generate revenue for charitable causes, among others. "NFTP" (non-fungible toilet paper) was christened by Charmin, and Taco Bell's NFT art sold out in minutes, with the top bids coming in at 1.5 wrapped ether (WETH), which is equivalent to $3,723.83 at the time of writing. Nyan Cat, a GIF depicting a cat with a pop-tart body that was created in 2011, sold for over $600,000 in February. In addition, as of late March, NBA Top Shot had produced more than $500 million in sales. A single LeBron James highlight NFT sold for more than $200,000 at an auction in New York. NFTs are being released by celebrities such as Snoop Dogg and Lindsay Lohan, who are offering unique memories, artwork, and experiences as securitized NFTs in order to raise money for charity.

How to create

In order to establish an NFT, we will first need to use a dApp (decentralized application). Anyone will be able to construct their own NFT with a few easy clicks thanks to the right dApp. Furthermore, the dApp will enable users to build a profile by just entering their name and email address into the application. For the user to be able to create a profile, however, the application needs to authenticate using Meta Mask. Once a person has created an account and been authorized, they may begin the process of creating their own NFT. Users must first provide a name, a description, and then choose a file in order to create the NFT. Once they have finished making their selections, all that is left is for them to click on the "Upload and Mint" option. A background upload function will be initiated, which will mint and upload the NFT to the blockchain as a result of this action. In contrast to other forms of cryptocurrency artwork, creating your own NFT artwork, whether it's in the form of a GIF or a picture, is a reasonably simple procedure that doesn't need substantial cryptographic understanding.

NFT artwork may also be utilized to produce collectibles such as sets of digital cards, which can be sold separately. In order to get started, you'll need to determine which blockchain you'll be using to issue your NFTs on. Ethereum is the blockchain service that is presently used for NFT issuance, and it is the most popular. Each blockchain has its own unique NFT token standard, as well as wallet services and markets that are compatible with it. For example, if you build NFTs on top of the Binance Smart Chain, you will only be able to sell them on exchanges that accept Binance Smart Chain assets as payment. This means you wouldn't be able to sell them on a marketplace like VIV3 – which is built on the Flow blockchain – or Open Sea, which is based on the Ethereum blockchain.

How to buy & sell

If you want to create your own NFT collection, you'll need to get your hands on a few essential products, which are as follows: It is necessary to first get a digital wallet that will enable you to store both NFTs and bitcoins. Depending on the currencies your NFT provider allows, you'll most likely need to acquire some cryptocurrency, like as Ether, to get started. You may now purchase cryptocurrency using a credit card on services such as Coinbase. After that, you'll be able to transfer it from the exchange to your preferred wallet of choice. When researching your alternatives, bear in mind that there are expenses to consider. When you acquire cryptocurrency, the majority of exchanges charge you at least a portion of your transaction.

Artists must either earn "upvotes" or an invitation to publish their work from other creators before they may do so. Because of the community's exclusivity and high barrier to entrance (artists must also acquire "gas" in order to mint NFTs), it is likely to have higher-quality artwork. For example, the developer of the Nyan Cat, sold the NFT on the Foundation platform. It might also result in higher pricing, which would not necessarily be a negative thing for artists and collectors looking to profit from the situation, providing that demand for NFTs continues at present levels or even grows over time. Despite the fact that these and other platforms are home to thousands of NFT makers and collectors, it is important to do thorough research before making a purchase. It has been reported that several artists have fallen prey to impersonators who have posted and sold their work without their consent. The verification methods for creators and NFT postings are also inconsistent among platforms, with some being more rigorous than others. NFT postings on sites like as Open Sea and Risible, for example, are not subject to owner verification requirements. While it comes to buying NFTs, buyer safeguards seem to be minimal at best, thus it may be advisable to remember the ancient adage "caveat emptor" (let the buyer beware) when purchasing.

Is it necessary to purchase NFTs just because they are available? It is situation-specific. Because the future of new financial technologies is unpredictable, and we don't yet have enough historical data to evaluate their effectiveness, they are hazardous. Because NFTs are so new, it's worth experimenting with them for a low cost right now. In other words, making the choice to invest in NFTs is mostly a personal one. If you have the means, it may be worthwhile to consider purchasing a piece, particularly if it has sentimental value to you. But bear in mind that the value of an NFT is totally dependent on how much someone else is prepared to pay for it. In this case, demand will drive the price rather than fundamental, technical or economic factors, which often impact crypto and stock prices and, at the very least, serve as the foundation for investor demand in the traditional sense. All of this implies that you may be able to resell your NFT for less than you paid for it. If no one is interested in buying it, you may be unable to resell it at all.

Similarly, to when you sell assets at a profit, NFTs are liable to capital gains taxes as well as ordinary income taxes. Because they are considered collectibles, they may not be eligible for the preferential long-term capital gains rates that apply to stocks, and they may even be subject to a higher collectibles tax rate, though it is not yet determined what constitutes a non-fungible transfer for taxation purposes. Keep in mind that the cryptocurrencies used to acquire the NFT may also be subject to taxation if their value has grown since you purchased them, so you may want to consult with a tax specialist before adding NFTs to your portfolio. That being stated, treat NFTs like you would any other kind of investment: Research the market thoroughly, understand the dangers (which include the possibility of losing all of your investment funds), and, if you decide to go forward, go with a healthy dosage of caution.

Biggest marketplaces

The top ten NFT marketplaces in terms of volume account for more than 90 percent of the total volume of NFT marketplaces. After recently announcing their intention to build a peer-to-peer NFT marketplace this year, Coinbase has already started a waiting list for anyone interested in participating. Recently, well-known industry brands like as FTX and Binance announced the creation of their own NFT markets. It is already evident that the largest crypto players will compete for market share in NFT, and it will be fascinating to watch what unique traits and USPs will be used to compensate for the success of the players. A genuine challenger, it seems, given the fact that Coinbase has 68 million wallets registered and that they do an excellent job of simplifying the user experience. Even while each NFT marketplace is distinct in its own manner, the underlying premise stays the same. Some are primarily concerned with art, while others are only concerned in collections.

Take a look at the top ten most active NFT markets by volume and see if we can find any similarities or differences. Open sea is unquestionably the most important of all the NFT markets right now, with an all-time volume of about $10 billion at the time this was written. In addition to NFTs, unique digital things, and crypto collectibles of all types, Open Sea also serves as a peer-to-peer marketplace for a variety of other products. NFTs may be discovered, purchased, sold, and auctioned. Sky Mavis's Axe Infinity is an NFT-based online video game produced by Vietnamese company Sky Mavis that makes use of the Ethereum-based cryptocurrencies AXS and SLP to fund its operations. The Axe infinite marketplace allows you to purchase, sell, and trade "Axis," which are virtual currency units. Play-to-earn paradigm is used in the game, in which users may earn a token that can be exchanged on Binance as an Ethereum-based cryptocurrency in exchange for their participation.

Players may also trade in-game assets for non-fungible tokens (NFTs) on the marketplace. Sky Mavis, the firm that produced Axe Infinity, raised $150 million in a Series B investment in October 2021, valuing the business at $3 billion. A16z was the lead investor in the deal. Using blockchain technology,

NBA Top Shot lets fans to purchase, sell, and trade numbered copies of particular, officially-licensed video highlights. The NBA trims the highlights, and then Dapper Labs selects how many copies of each clip they will sell and numbers them accordingly. In the same way that real trading cards are packaged, they package each highlight into a digital pack, which they then sell on the official NBA Top Shot website for prices ranging from $9 to $230. It is dependent on the quality of the highlight, the fame of the player and the exclusivity of the card on which the pack is based on the price of the card. The highlights from the pack are stored in your encrypted, safe highlight wallet where they may be "showcased" or resold on the NBA Top Shot Marketplace once you acquire them. Risible is an Ethereum-based platform that allows users to create, sell, and acquire ownership rights to digital works of art via the use of non-fungible tokens (NFTs).

The RARI token is intended to empower community members by giving them the ability to define the platform's future, curate, moderate, and vote on new features and functionality. Risible distributes governance tokens using a process known as "marketplace mining," in which 75,000 RARI are distributed equally between buyers and sellers each week. Super Rare is an online marketplace for the purchase and exchange of one-of-a-kind, limited-edition digital artworks. Each piece of artwork is truly generated by a member of the network and tokenized as a crypto-collectible digital object that you can own and trade with other members of the network. Super Rare may be thought of as a cross between Instagram and Christie's. Soarer is a football-themed fantasy game in which players purchase, sell, trade, and manage a virtual team comprised of digital player cards. Soarer is a blockchain-based platform that allows gamers to manage virtual teams of five football players made out of blockchain cards. Teams are rated according to the performance of their players on a real-world soccer field, and points are awarded to them in the same way that regular fantasy football is. In October 2021, Soarer raised a record-breaking $680 million in a single financing.

Worldwide Developments

As the cryptocurrency market continues to soar after a great start, it is possible that the future will be no different. While some countries have had tough stances on cryptocurrencies (in some cases banning them), other countries have taken a completely opposite approach – by fully legalizing cryptocurrencies.

By their very nature, cryptocurrencies are decentralized. This means that no central entity or authority has control over them. Thus, this protects these currencies to a certain degree from being banned. Furthermore, since they are not tied to any particular nation's economy, the value of cryptocurrencies is based on what investors are willing to pay for it at a given time. This makes the cryptocurrency market highly volatile and unpredictable.

Cryptocurrencies are an intriguing notion that has the potential to profoundly transform the global financial system for the better if properly implemented. However, despite the fact that it is founded on strong, democratic ideas, many cryptocurrencies are still considered a technical and practical development project. The near-monopoly that nation-states have on money creation and monetary policy looks to be safe for the foreseeable future. In the meanwhile, crypto investors should maintain constant awareness of the concept's practical limits. Any claims that a certain cryptocurrency provides complete anonymity or freedom from legal liability should be treated with extreme suspicion, just as claims that specific cryptocurrencies provide flawless investment possibilities or inflation hedges should be treated with extreme caution. Look at gold which is often referred to be the "ultimate inflation hedge," it is nonetheless vulnerable to extreme volatility - much more than the fiat currencies of many industrialized nations.

Gold and cryptocurrencies are both in the same boat, albeit in entirely different vessels. Gold is a tangible asset with a history dating back to the earliest civilizations. It was money before currency existed and has maintained its value through thousands of years despite economic and political upheavals and fluctuations in demand due to wars, recessions or natural disasters.

On the other hand, cryptocurrencies are virtual and do not exist as a physical commodity. They can be mined or traded online and they generate value through the shared agreement of market participants who regard them as valuable. Their scarcity is predetermined, and new coins cannot be created beyond what is already planned.

As a conclusion, it can be said that cryptocurrencies and gold share many similarities and yet, they both have their own unique merits and demerits. While cryptocurrencies may be in vogue at the moment, it remains to be seen how much longer this will last and what type of impact these virtual currencies will have on the world economy in the future.

In any case, sensible investors should not get overly excited or distraught about a particular investment vehicle or concept – be it a cryptocurrency, a stock, a house, gold or even an investment in one's education. Do not put all of your eggs into one basket – no matter the investment, it is always a good idea to maintain a well-diversified portfolio for a well-rounded financial future.

Outlook and Conclusion

The cryptocurrency market has shown impressive growth in the past years, with Bitcoin and Ethereum experiencing a tenfold increase in price and many other currencies following suit. However, it's not just these top currencies that show promise; hundreds of lesser-known cryptocurrencies have been showing similar upward trends, and investors who get in now may be rewarded with substantial gains.

Crypto as an investment asset class is still very young; Bitcoin was invented only a decade ago, and the market is mostly unregulated, so it's volatile by nature. Even so, many pundits have claimed that investing in cryptocurrency will soon replace traditional investments such as stocks and bonds. This may well be true, but for now cryptocurrency is still an excellent investment opportunity, especially if you are able to get in before it reaches wider adoption.

The main factors that affect the price of a cryptocurrency are supply and demand, meaning if more people want to buy than sell, the currency will rise in value. Technological advancement like breakthroughs in hardware or software can influence whether or not crypto is adopted by major players such as banks and governments. This would obviously boost its price stability since a cryptocurrency that is regularly used as a medium of exchange, and has a good market cap and supply will tend to be more stable than others. This makes it suitable for short-term investments or as a means of storing wealth.

Cryptocurrencies have been called the "Internet's native currency", so clearly those with an internet connection can trade them. However, it's important to bear in mind that the internet is not an "equal opportunity" medium. People living in repressive regimes may have a hard time accessing crypto exchanges. This may change as cryptocurrency becomes more mainstream, but for now it's important to be aware of this aspect before committing large sums of money to it.

Of course, the biggest risk of any investment is not getting your money back. While it may be possible to lose money on an individual cryptocurrency, diversifying between multiple coins will help even out the blows and reduce the risks. It's also important to invest only what you can afford to lose. Some currencies are considered "shitcoins" by some investors; while they may have a low market cap and be priced accordingly, this doesn't mean they can't rise to the same heights as the older currencies. The key is due diligence – do your research before you invest, and don't just buy something because it appears cheap.

I hope that you liked this book and it was helpful for you to get started with investing in cryptocurrency. Now that you know how it works, go out there and invest!

Please feel free to share it with your friends and family if you feel that they need it.

Thank You and good luck!

www.ingramcontent.com/pod-product-compliance
Lightning Source LLC
LaVergne TN
LVHW081536060526
838200LV00048B/2096